# SLOW COOK SOLAR

# SLOW COOK SOLAR

## Sun-Baked Summer Meals Good for People and Planet

Lorraine Anderson

Photographs by Philip M. Lew

GREEN HERON PRESS
Corvallis, OR

"Slower, it turns out, often means better—better health, better work, better business, better family life, better exercise, *better cuisine*..."

—Carl Honoré, *In Praise of Slow*

# Contents

*Summertime, and the livin' is easy.*

# PREFACE:
# The Gift of Sunshine

**WHEN THE SUN** gets high enough in the sky to bathe a corner of the back deck in sunshine most of the day—about mid-May in Oregon—I know it's time to put the Crock-Pot away and pull the solar cooker out. The livin' is about to get easy. Slow cooking outdoors using only the energy of the sun is simple, safe, and free. It creates no pollution and keeps your kitchen cool. It's a brilliant way to prepare seasonal, local, organic, whole (SLOW) foods, the basis of a regenivore diet—a diet that supports the health of our soil, our communities, our planet, and ourselves.

Most Americans, including those who live in Seattle, Minneapolis, Boston, and New York City, can cook with sunshine all summer long. In fact, you can cook with sunshine if you live anywhere between the 60th parallels of latitude on planet Earth. This means almost everywhere in the world except for Greenland, Iceland, the Scandinavian countries, and the northernmost reaches of Canada and Russia. The closer you are to the equator, the more solar cooking days you'll have.

To get started, you'll need a solar cooker that you purchase or make, along with one or more thin-walled, dark-colored pots with lids. You'll also need a few square feet in your yard, on your driveway, on a balcony or deck, or on your rooftop where you get full sunshine in the summer for most of the day.

And you'll need a few good recipes. The ones you'll find here have been carefully curated for flavor, nutrient-dense whole food ingredients, and simplicity. Most are vegan or vegetarian, for a plant-rich plate; a few use chicken, beef, or seafood as an accent. The majority are gluten free and emphasize fresh fruits and vegetables from the garden or farmers market.

Enjoy the adventure of learning to use the gift of sunshine to make summer cooking easy, delicious, and regenerative. *Bon appetit!* ☼

# Your Solar-Powered Slow Cooker

## "OKAY, I'M HOOKED!"

My friend Sheridan had been curious about solar cooking. She unpacked her new Haines 2.0 solar panel cooker and placed a pound of raw new potatoes in the included Dutch oven with some butter, garlic powder, paprika, salt, and pepper. She started cooking at 8:30 AM one fine May day in Oregon and had a perfectly done dish by lunchtime.

"You got me, Lorraine. I'm a convert. Thank you for introducing me to this whole new world. I feel simultaneously righteous and like I'm totally getting away with something," she emailed me.

Bingo! Another score for personal and planetary health. You can join the team too. With a little preliminary info and the right gear, you'll be ready to harvest the considerable benefits of cooking with sunshine.

## HOW SOLAR COOKING WORKS

Solar cooking, a proven technology that has long been employed around the world, uses only the radiant energy of sunshine to cook food. A reflector pointed toward the sun focuses the rays on a dark vessel, which absorbs those rays and turns them into heat. The heat is trapped and held around the vessel by a glass or plastic cover. You're familiar with this phenomenon from getting into your car when it's been parked in a sunny spot.

Solar cookers come in a variety of shapes and sizes, but the simplest are panel and box cookers. They can be made of cardboard or more durable materials. Panel cookers have shiny surfaces that direct sunshine onto dark-colored lidded cookware enclosed in a clear insulating shell like a plastic oven bag or an inverted glass bowl. This insulating shell lets in the sunlight and then holds in the heat that's generated by the sunlight touching the dark pot. Box cookers have hinged reflector tops that direct sunshine onto dark-colored lidded cookware. A transparent window of glass or plastic on the box keeps the heat in.

These cookers are safe and easy to use, relatively inexpensive, and readily available. You can prepare all the recipes in this book using a panel or box cooker.

The simplest panel cookers heat food to between 200 and 250 degrees F. (Food cooks at 180 degrees F, and water boils at 212 degrees F.) More elaborate panel and box cookers cause food to reach higher temperatures. By way of comparison, food in a Crock-Pot reaches a maximum temperature at or just below the boiling point, sooner if set on high, later if set on low.

## WHY IT'S GOOD FOR YOU AND THE PLANET

Solar cooking is a natural for preparing seasonal, local, organic, and whole (SLOW) foods. A diet of such foods, particularly if it's rich in plants, can reduce $CO_2$ emissions as well as support the health of our soil, our communities, and ourselves.

The best diet for human and planetary health maximizes plant foods and minimizes

*A panel cooker with a clear plastic insulating shell, the Haines 1.0.*

# INGREDIENTS FOR A HEALTHY PLATE

*Most of the recipes in this book use fresh whole foods, preferably organic and local. Ingredients freshly picked from your garden or bought at the farmers market get a big thumbs up. For recipes that use dairy, poultry, eggs, or meat, I prefer organic, local, and pasture raised, grass fed, or free range. These choices support food producers who improve the soil, raise animals humanely, and respect workers. For recipes that use seafood, I consult the Monterey Bay Aquarium Seafood Watch site (seafoodwatch.org) for best choices.*

*Lots of different substitutions are possible to meet your dietary needs and preferences. Nondairy cheeses can be substituted for dairy cheeses, and the same thing with yogurt and milk.*

*I like to use coconut oil to grease pans before baking, since it stays on the sides. For salad dressings, I use extra virgin olive oil or avocado oil. For baking, avocado oil.*

*When a sweetener is necessary, I avoid cane sugar and instead use maple syrup, honey, stevia, coconut sugar, xylitol, or granulated monk fruit. Honey and maple syrup can be used pretty much interchangeably, although Ayurveda tells us that heating honey to 104 degrees F causes undesirable chemical changes. I use stevia if it's in a flavor mix where it doesn't taste too artificial, as in Mexican Chocolate Pudding.*

animal foods. According to the EAT-*Lancet* Commission (thelancet.com/commissions/EAT), "A diet rich in plant-based foods and with fewer animal-source foods confers both improved health and environmental benefits." A plant-rich diet ranks #4 and clean cookstoves #21 in *Drawdown*, the 2017 book edited by Paul Hawken that catalogs the hundred most substantive solutions to reverse climate change.

Clearly, a plant-rich diet cooked with sunshine and thus producing no emissions is good for the planet, and it's also good for your health, your taste buds, and your pocketbook.

According to Blue Zones, the longest-lived people in the world consume a mainly plant-based diet, eat seasonally, and cook at home. Following the recipes in this book will help you do the same. If you occasionally eat meat (preferably local, organic, and grass fed) as a modest part of a plant-rich diet, cooking it with sunshine is healthier than grilling, which can produce cancer-causing chemicals (heterocyclic amines and polycyclic aromatic hydrocarbons).

The secret ingredient for the best-tasting and most nutritious food turns out to be time. As slow cooking enthusiasts already know, slow cooking amplifies flavors and preserves nutrients. This is as true for vegetables as it is for meats. Cooking veggies longer makes them a sweeter, deeper version of themselves (see "The Best Way to Cook Vegetables: Low and Slow," a June 2021 article in the *New York Times Magazine* by Tejal Rao). Cooking meats slowly with sunshine enhances tenderness and flavor by giving muscle fibers ample time to break down and slowly transform into gelatin.

Your initial investment in a solar box or panel cooker can be less than $100, or you can make it yourself for the cost of materials. There are no moving parts that might break and require costly repairs. The energy is 100 percent free, so you save on your gas or electricity bill. And because it doesn't heat up your kitchen on a hot day, you save on air-conditioning costs.

## THE BEST SOLAR COOKER FOR YOU

To get started with solar cooking, you'll need to make or buy a box or panel cooker. You can begin with an inexpensive model and then upgrade once you've gotten into the habit of cooking summer meals with the sun. I started out with a cardboard box cooker I made myself, then cooked for a dozen years with a simple cardboard panel cooker (the Solar CooKit). Only then did I invest in a Solavore Sport box cooker (sadly, no longer available). Later I added a Haines 1.0, a Haines 2.0, a Copenhagen, and an All Season Solar Cooker.

Solar cookers are available for purchase in most areas of the world and online. More solar cooker models are for sale every year, and I expect that trend to continue as the benefits of solar cooking become more widely known.

The best solar cooker for you depends on what your needs are. If you're just getting started, you may want a cooker that's less expensive and takes up little storage space. The Solar CooKit or the Copenhagen could be just what you want.

The **Solar CooKit** is a cardboard panel cooker that's so easy to fold flat for storage that you can stow it indoors every evening. It was the first panel cooker ever developed, by a team at Solar Cookers International. The CooKit will cook any recipe in this book and last for many years if you keep it out of the rain. It includes a sturdy transparent heat-resistant oven bag to hold heat around a dark cooking vessel you provide. *Available at solarcookers.org/resources/cookit-purchase.*

The **Copenhagen** is a very affordable, lightweight, compact, portable panel cooker made of four reflective vinyl squares (waterproof!) that can easily be taken apart and folded flat for storage, though not as easily as the CooKit. You can use turkey-size oven bags from the grocery store to enclose dark lidded cookware. *Order the Copenhagen from oursuncooks.com.*

If you want a very sturdy panel cooker that's designed to maximize the number of hours and the length of the season during which you can cook, the **All Season Solar Cooker** could be the one. This rugged and roomy unit is made of corrugated polypropylene with an aluminum surface (waterproof!). It's highly adjustable and has a unique aiming device and an open front that makes it easy to scoop up every last ray of sun for an extended cooking day or season. You can use turkey-size oven bags from the grocery store or clear glass bowls to enclose dark lidded cookware. The cooker is somewhat challenging to assemble so you'll want to leave it up all season, but then it can be disassembled to store over the winter in a compact cardboard box. *Find it at solcook.com and on Amazon.*

*The Solar CooKit from Solar Cookers International, a good beginning solar cooker.*

If you want a happy medium between cooking power and portability, you may love the **Haines 2.0 SunUp Solar Cooker** as much as I do. The Haines 2.0 is a lightweight and efficient panel cooker made of Mylar bonded to polyester foam (waterproof!) that snaps together for quick assembly and disassembly, and rolls up to fit in a yoga mat bag. A circular flexible plastic cover keeps warm air around your dark lidded pot, and a plastic standoff holds the pot up so sunshine can be reflected onto the bottom too. *The 2.0 model is available with or without a 4.5-quart stainless steel cooking pot at hainessolarcookers.com and on Amazon.*

A mid-priced durable solar panel cooker to consider is the **HotPot** from Solar Household Energy. The HotPot combines a pot assembly with a metal panel arrangement much like the CooKit. The pot assembly consists of a 5-liter (about 5 quarts) black enameled steel pot supported by its rim inside a clear glass bowl with a glass lid. The space between the pot and the bowl creates a greenhouse that retains heat. *Order at she-inc.org.*

Box ovens generally reach higher temperatures than panel cookers but are more expensive and require more storage space because they can't be broken down. My favorite box oven, which cost me around $220 in 2014, is the **Solavore Sport**, made of recycled nylon resin (no BPAs) and large

## COOKER INFORMATION AND PLANS

*The Solar Cookers International (SCI) Solar Cooking Wiki (solarcooking.org or solarcooking.fandom.com) is the most comprehensive and up-to-date online source of cooker information, plans, and links to models for sale.*

*Solar Cookers: How to Make, Use, and Enjoy, 10th ed. (58 pages, 2004), available free from SCI, shows how to make panel and box cookers and also gives recipes, tips, and a brief history of solar cooking. It can be downloaded from: solarcooking.org/plans/plans.pdf.*

enough to fit two Granite Ware roasting pans side by side. *Sadly, production ceased in 2019. If you can find one used, grab it.*

If you're in it for the long haul and don't mind spending more for a heavier oven that reaches temperatures more like your indoor oven, the **All American Sun Oven** (sunoven.com) may be the answer. To go even more all-in, consider the **SunFocus Solar Electric Oven** (sunbdcorp.com), which offers the option of plugging in to cook outdoors with electricity on cloudy days or at night. *Both of these cookers are available on Amazon.*

Dedicated solar cooks may also be attracted to the elegance and efficiency of a more recent entry, the **Suntaste** box cooker by the Portuguese firm SunOK (sunok.eu). The Suntaste is made of cork for its excellent insulating qualities, its light weight, and its sustainability (cork is a renewable resource, and cork trees sequester carbon while growing the bark layer that is harvested without hurting the tree). *The Suntaste is available in two different sizes and can be ordered by emailing info@sunok.eu.*

A word about parabolic and evacuated tube solar cookers. Both types are available online at Walmart (as well as Amazon and other vendors), which is a step toward solar cookers achieving parity with backyard barbecues, something I heartily applaud. One of these models may be right for your needs, but they have drawbacks that make them less appealing to the average cook, so this cookbook doesn't specifically apply to them.

Parabolic cookers reach very high temperatures but need constant tending and repositioning in the hot sun, and they tend to be bulky, heavy, and expensive. The Haines 2.0 cooker I love is considered by its inventor, Roger Haines, to be a "panelbolic" design, combining the best of panel and parabolic cookers.

Evacuated tube cookers, exemplified by the Glenergy Solar Cooker (glenergy.ca), Fornelia cookers (fornelia.com), the GoSun line (gosun.co), and a number of Chinese knockoffs, can be handy for picnics and camping but require careful handling. A cooking drawer slides out so it can be loaded with raw food, then slides back into the tube. Check this out for yourself if you think it might be the answer to your needs.

## THE RIGHT COOKWARE AND TOOLS

The ideal solar cookware is dark to absorb and hold heat, and thin to heat up quickly. It's short and wide rather than tall and deep, to ensure the contents cook all the way through. Nontoxic surfaces such as glass, porcelain enamel, ceramic, and stainless steel are preferable to safeguard your health. Well-fitting lids, either dark or clear, keep steam from escaping that might cloud the insulating shell or box window and cut down on the sunshine coming in. Clear tempered glass lids have the advantage of allowing you to check the progress of your food without removing the lid, plus they retain heat better than metal lids.

Granite Ware checks all the boxes. This cookware is made of speckled black or brown porcelain enamel over carbon steel. The covered roasting pans from this company are affordable and widely available in stores like Target and on Amazon, and they last a long time. Get yourself a couple of 3-pound (9-3/4-inch-round, 3-quart-capacity) covered roaster pans to get started. The only drawback to these pans is that if you chip the porcelain, the underlying carbon steel can rust.

A 4.5-quart stainless steel pot with a black exterior and a glass lid is offered for sale either packaged with the Haines 2.0 SunUp Solar Cooker or separately at hainessolarcookers.com. This is a highly versatile solar cooking vessel that lets you see what's going on in the pot. I especially like baking bread in it.

A dark 5-by-10-inch loaf pan, a dark 7-by-11-inch brownie pan, and a dark 8- or 9-inch-square cake pan are also useful pieces of cookware to have on hand as you get started with solar cooking.

*The best all-around pan for solar cooking: the Granite Ware 3-pound roaster (9-3/4 inches round, 3-quart capacity), shown here with ingredients for Chipotle Red Pepper Bisque ready to cook.*

Inexpensive gray nonstick baking pans may seem like the perfect solar cooking solution because they're dark and thin and thus heat up well, but I've found that they degrade pretty quickly with normal use. The coating on those pans is bad news when it flakes off or is scratched by metal utensils. Pans with a dark ceramic coating are a better bet; CasaWare, Gotham Steel, and Granitestone are durable brands that are widely available.

Dark stoneware is a surprisingly good option. It heats up more slowly than thinner metal pans but also holds the heat longer, plus it's nontoxic, and I've gotten a lot of use out of my 9-inch-square dark blue lidded ceramic pan for baking brownies, lasagna, and casseroles. You may wonder about using your cast iron skillet or Dutch oven. Like stoneware, cast iron takes longer to heat up than lighter materials but also holds

*Baking nuts in a Haines 1.0 (left), green beans in a Copenhagen (middle), and lasagna in a Solavore Sport (right).*

heat longer. Experiment with it in your solar cooker and find out what happens.

Anodized aluminum and carbon steel bakeware are also workable choices. I would avoid silicone bakeware; even though it's been approved by the FDA, it hasn't been studied enough to know definitively whether it leaches toxins into your food.

A couple of clear 4-quart Pyrex mixing bowls make a nifty insulating shell around dark cookware for use in panel cookers. Search for Cookware Demo 480 by Jim La Joie on YouTube to see a demonstration of the many ingenious ways to combine cookware for use in his All Season Solar Cooker as well as other panel cookers.

A blender comes in handy to make salad dressings and sauces and to make soups from veggies that have been solar cooked until nicely soft. A handheld immersion blender is ideal for the latter use and saves you the trouble of transferring ingredients into and out of a blender container. The handheld blender also gives you a little bit of a chunkier result, which is nice for many veggie soups. ☀

## THE IDEAL SOLAR BAKEWARE SET

*After decades of solar cooking I've assembled what I consider the ideal collection of dark pans for making every recipe in this book. I use these year-round, in the indoor oven during the winter as well. Here's what I've got:*

- **2 black 3-pound Granite Ware roasters with lids**

- **1 black 4.5-quart stainless steel Dutch oven with clear glass lid**

- **1 dark blue 9-by-9-inch stoneware pan with lid**

- **1 dark gray ceramic-coated 7-by-11-inch brownie pan**

- **1 dark blue ceramic-coated 5-by-10-inch loaf pan**

- **1 black nonstick 9-by-13-inch roaster pan**

# Tips and Techniques

**COOKING WITH THE SUN IS EASY.**
Think Crock-Pot and prep the dish the night before or the morning of the day you want to serve it for lunch or dinner. Put it in the solar cooker by midmorning (or for easier-to-cook foods, by lunchtime or midafternoon) and let the sun go to work. When it's time to eat, take your fully cooked food out of the cooker and do some last-minute finishing touches.

Here are the key things to know and do.

**START SIMPLE AND RESOLVE TO NOT GIVE UP.** Try out solar cooking on weekends before doing it every day. Start with beets or potatoes to prove to yourself that you don't have heat up the kitchen to have perfectly done ingredients for a beet or potato salad (see the recipes for Beet and Blueberry Salad with Gorgonzola, Sour Cream Dill Potato Salad, and Adobo Potato Salad). Or start with dessert, since life is short. The recipes in this book for Black Bean Brownies, Summer Fruit Crumble, and Mexican Chocolate Pudding are particularly easy and rewarding.

Don't be afraid; just dive in and give it a go. Experimentation is the name of the game. Once you've had a few successes and realize the magic of this new skill you're adding to your summer cooking repertoire, you'll become bolder about what you attempt.

**LEARN TO PLAN AHEAD.** Solar cooking is about slow food, in contrast to the fast or just-in-time food habit you may have fallen into. At first it may seem hard to think a day ahead about what you're going to eat for dinner, but once you do it a few times it becomes easier, and eventually it's second nature. The beauty of cooking with sunshine during the summer is that the long hours of daylight make it easier to get up early and prep your evening meal. You can also do it the evening before.

You might even try thinking and cooking a week ahead. For instance, on a sunny Sunday, if you know you're going to make Adobo Potato Salad, Glory Bowls, and Fiesta Chicken Salad during the week ahead, you can solar cook the red potatoes, beets, and chicken breasts you're going to use and keep them in the fridge until the day you use them. Cold veggie soups (a great way to use the oversupply that sometimes strikes the best-planned garden) are most refreshing served thoroughly chilled, so that means making them the day before or else refrigerating the cooked veggies overnight and then adding the finishing touches just before eating.

## KNOW YOUR PRIME COOKING SEASON.

The closer to the equator you live, the more prime cooking days you'll have. You can probably use your solar cooker for a number of weeks before and after the prime cooking season in your part of the world, especially for easier-to-cook foods. If you live near or south of 40 degrees N latitude (the 40th parallel north)—the approximate latitude of Reno, Salt Lake City, Denver, Kansas City, Indianapolis, Columbus, Wheeling, and Philadelphia—you have at least 150 prime solar cooking days a year, between mid-April and mid-September. South of 35 degrees N latitude (the 35th parallel north)—in southern

## FOOD SAFETY

*Food safety is not a big concern if you observe a few commonsense guidelines. Microbiologists who have made a careful study of solar cooking have documented that it's safe to put raw refrigerated or frozen food, even chicken or other meat, in a solar cooker in the morning several hours before the sun begins to cook it. The food remains cold enough to prevent germ growth until the sun starts to heat the cooker. Then the food heats up quickly to the point where harmful food microbes, including bacteria and viruses, are killed—at 160 degrees F, the point at which food is pasteurized. (Water pasteurizes at 150 degrees F.)*

*If you're cooking any food that's not safe to eat when it's raw and you want to be absolutely sure, use a food thermometer to check for doneness. The US Department of Agriculture advises that poultry and casseroles should reach a minimum internal temperature of 165 degrees F to be safe to eat. For eggs and ground meats, it's 160 degrees F. For seafood and large cuts of meat, at least 145 degrees F. Foods easily*

*reach this temperature when cooked in a dark pan in even the simplest panel cookers.*

*You do need to be aware of how long food sits in the solar cooker after the sun leaves it. The general guideline from the Centers for Disease Control is that food (especially meats) should not be left in the danger zone below 140 degrees F and above 40 degrees F for more than 2 hours. Breads and fruit pies are the exception to this rule. If you do find that you've left a dish in the solar cooker for more than 2 hours after direct sun leaves it, you may want to play it safe by composting it and reaching for that frozen dinner you've kept on hand for an emergency.*

*If you're cooking something that will be finished an hour or more before dinnertime and you'd like to stop the cooking but keep it in the safe zone above 140 degrees F, you can put the pot or pan in an insulated container to hold until you're ready to eat. An ice chest (or a basket) lined with a small blanket or quilt will do the trick.*

California, Arizona, New Mexico, Texas, and the Deep South—you can use your solar cooker for half the year or more.

### FIND THE RIGHT LOCATION FOR YOUR COOKER.

Find a spot for your solar cooker where it will remain in full sun most of the day. A hard, flat, level surface is best, like a deck, patio, balcony, rooftop, sidewalk, or driveway. You can also put it on a table for easier access and to keep it out of reach of curious animals. (Most animals won't disturb it since the cooking pot is hot.) Also find a safe place to stow your cooker when the cooking is done so it doesn't get dusty, blown over, or rained on.

### WAIT FOR A CLEAR, SUNNY—OR AT LEAST PARTLY SUNNY—DAY.

To cook with sunshine, you need, well, sunshine. On a prime solar cooking day, the sun is high (45 degrees or more above the horizon) for 4 hours or more. When your shadow is shorter than your height, the sun is high enough in the sky to cook successfully.

But don't let a few clouds keep you from solar cooking. You *can* cook on a partly cloudy day. You need to see the sun for just 20 minutes out of every hour to get the energy you need to hold temperatures high. If you're not sure or if a heavy cloud cover moves in before your food is fully cooked, bring it inside and finish cooking it in the oven. Remember that you don't want partially cooked foods—especially meats—to remain in the danger zone between 40 and 140 degrees F for more than 2 hours.

### SCOOP THE PRIME SOLAR COOKING HOURS.

The prime solar cooking hours are 10 AM to 3 PM, when the sun is highest in the sky, and you should be sure your harder-to-cook foods (root vegetables, brown rice, beans) are in the oven during those hours at least. On the longest summer days, you can start things earlier and keep them cooking later if need be.

Your food will stay hotter if the cooker is always facing directly into the sun. For faster cooking, plan to readjust the cooker every 30 minutes to maintain the highest temperatures. This isn't necessary for solar cooking to work, though. Just put your food in when the sun has started to hit your cooker and turn the cooker so it faces the spot where the sun will be at midday.

### RAISE THE POT UP.

In a box or panel cooker, raising the pot or pan inside the oven bag or oven chamber by placing it on a metal rack or trivet or on a clear glass bowl or pie pan improves cooker performance. It allows heated air to circulate all the way around the pot or pan. The Haines 2.0 SunUp Solar Cooker comes with a plastic cooking sleeve that raises your pot or pan up, contributing to this cooker's efficiency and ability to reach higher temperatures than other panel cookers.

## STACK POTS OR USE MULTIPLE COOKERS FOR MULTIPLE DISHES.
You can put as many pots in your cooker as space allows. You can stack one pot on top of another if one has a flat lid. Or you can use more than one cooker if you want to cook multiple dishes. Put foods with longer cooking times and/or in larger pots to the back of a box cooker where more sun will reach them.

## DON'T PEEK; DON'T STIR.
There's no need to take the lid off once you start cooking a dish unless you think it's nearly done and want to check. Taking the lid off will let heat out and slow down cooking, just as for a slow cooker. This is why glass lids are great for the view they give you. You don't need to stir anything—even polenta!—for it to come out perfectly. Take your pot holders with you when you go to check dishes or get the food out of the cooker. Sunglasses can cut the glare coming off a shiny surface in the sunshine.

## YOUR TEMPERATURES MAY VARY, SO COOKING TIMES ARE ALWAYS APPROXIMATE.
The temperatures your cooker reaches do *not* depend on the ambient air temperature. They depend on

## TYPICAL COOKING TIMES

*Chicken and fish, egg-and-cheese dishes, easier-to-cook grains like quinoa and buckwheat groats, fruit, and aboveground vegetables cook in 1 to 2 hours and may start to dry out if left in longer.*

*Lentils, most grains, and breads take 2 to 4 hours to cook and can be left in longer without negative consequences.*

*Whole root vegetables (potatoes, beets, carrots, onions, and such) and dried beans need 4 to 6 hours or longer to cook thoroughly and can stay in the cooker untended all day.*

*The more food you put in a pot, the larger the pieces of food are, and the more pots you put in your solar cooker, the more slowly the food cooks.*

*It's nearly impossible to burn anything, so if you get held up and can't bring a dish inside at the ideal time, it won't be inedible or stuck to the pot. This is especially true for more forgiving foods like root vegetables, moist meats, and soups and stews.*

the type of cooker you're using, the type of cooking vessel, the angle of the sun, how much haze is in the sky, how close you are to the equator, the time of day, and how often you re-aim your cooker toward the sun's rays.

The cooking times given in this book apply to cooking in full sun during the prime solar cooking hours of 10 AM to 3 PM during the summer months. If you're cooking on a hazy or partly cloudy day, outside the prime cooking hours, or outside the prime cooking season, when the sun is lower in the sky, adjust your time expectation upward.

Your own experience is the best guide. Through trial and error, you'll soon get a feel for how long things take and whether you need to put them in first thing in the morning or can wait and prep them at lunchtime.

## TROUBLESHOOT WHAT'S NOT WORKING.

If your food doesn't cook, the problem is in one of four areas: collection, absorption, retention, or duration. To collect the sun's rays, the cooker must be pointed toward the sun and receive full sun in the prime cooking hours between 10 AM and 3 PM. Are shadows encroaching on your cooking area as the

*Mind the shadows and make sure your cooker stays in full sun when something's baking.*

day progresses? To absorb the sun's rays, your cooking pot must be dark (unless you're cooking dark cake or cookie batter) and ideally have thin walls and a tight-fitting lid. To retain the heat, your cooking bag or cover should enclose the pot or pan but leave room around the pot or pan for air to circulate. As far as duration, you should allow enough time for cooking during the prime cooking hours.

## ADAPT YOUR OWN FAVORITE RECIPES TO THE SOLAR COOKER. Along with following the recipes in this book, try adapting your own favorite recipes. Crock-Pot or slow cooker recipes work well. Remember that what a solar cooker does best is to cook food that appreciates long, slow cooking and can generate enough internal moisture to stay moist and tender. To adapt a conventional recipe to the solar cooker, adjust the cooking time and the amount of liquid. Dishes take roughly twice as long to bake in a solar cooker and use less liquid than in a conventional oven. If you're adding chopped onions or other hard-to-cook foods to a solar dish, you may want to finely grate them or else saute them on the stovetop first.

## CARE FOR YOUR COOKER. Your cooker will last longer if you treat it well. That means moving it to a shady spot after you've finished

## KEEP THE FLAVORS GOING AFTER SUMMER ENDS

*If you're like me, you're gonna love some of these recipes so much that you don't want to give them up just because summer comes to an end and you put your solar cooker away. You can adapt the recipes in this book to indoor cooking in the winter. If you want to get the health and flavor benefits of cooking at lower temperatures, set your indoor oven to anywhere between 200 and 250 degrees F, depending on whether you're most interested in keeping the food really tender (the lower temperature) or getting it to brown and cook faster (the higher temperature). If you're most interested in speed, you can turn your oven to between 325 and 350 degrees F and cut the cooking time in half.*

cooking for the day so that it doesn't sit out in the sun empty, since sunlight tends to degrade materials. If it's cardboard, move it indoors at the first smell of rain. At the end of the season, disassemble and clean it up with a damp rag or sponge, then tuck it away out of the elements—in your garage, basement, attic, garden shed, pantry, or storage locker—until summer rolls around again. ☀

# Pestos, Spreads, and Breads

*Applesauce Oat Bread*

# GREEN BEAN PESTO

MAKES about 1-1/2 cups | COOK 2 to 3 hours | **GLUTEN FREE, VEGAN**

*Once the green beans in the garden start ripening, I use this recipe a lot. Solar cooking makes the beans soft enough to blend while deepening their flavor. It doesn't preserve their crispness or bright green color, but that doesn't matter in this recipe. I love this pesto on crackers.*

### Into the cooker:
2 cups (about 8 ounces) green beans that have been trimmed and cut into 1-inch lengths

### Into the blender:
1/3 cup toasted pecan pieces
1/4 cup avocado oil
1/2 teaspoon salt
1 or 2 cloves garlic, coarsely chopped

1. Place the green beans in a dark baking pan. Cover and bake in the solar cooker until tender when tested with a fork, 2 to 3 hours. Allow to cool.

2. In a blender, puree the green beans with the pecan pieces, oil, salt, and garlic until smooth. Scrape into a bowl to serve or store in the fridge.

# BEET PESTO

MAKES about 2 cups | COOK 4 to 6 hours | **GLUTEN FREE, VEGETARIAN**

*People don't know what to make of the bright pink color of this pesto, but when they taste it, they agree it's a delicious way to eat beets. I like to spread it on corn or rice thins and top it with slices of avocado as an appetizer (or lunch). It's also delicious on pasta or potatoes. Solar cooking is the absolutely best and easiest way to prepare beets. Just put them in the cooker and leave them all day. Cook up a batch to use in more than one dish or to put in your smoothie at lunchtime.*

**Into the cooker:**

2 medium beets, greens and roots trimmed off

**Into the blender:**

1/2 cup olive oil
1/4 cup pine nuts
2 tablespoons chopped fresh basil
2 tablespoons fresh lemon juice
1/2 teaspoon salt
1 or 2 cloves garlic, coarsely chopped

**Stir in:**

1/2 cup grated Parmesan cheese

1. Place the beets in a dark baking pan. Cover and bake in the solar cooker until tender when tested with a fork, 4 to 6 hours or longer. Allow to cool, and then rub off the peel with a paper towel. Slice large chunks into a blender.

2. In the blender, puree the beets with the oil, pine nuts, basil, lemon juice, salt, and garlic until smooth.

3. Stir in the Parmesan cheese. Scrape into a bowl to serve or store in the fridge.

# EGGPLANT-TAHINI SPREAD

MAKES about 2 cups  |  COOK 2 to 3 hours  |  **GLUTEN FREE, VEGAN**

*Eggplant gets beautifully soft in the solar cooker, perfect for blending into this flavorful spread. I use parsley fresh from the garden and appreciate how it tones down the garlic breath that would otherwise result. Serve this spread on pita bread and garnish with chopped tomato, sliced cucumber, and/or crumbled feta cheese for a light lunch, or just dip into it with pita chips.*

### Into the cooker:
1 large eggplant, peeled and
    cut into large cubes

### Into the blender:
3 tablespoons fresh lemon juice
3 tablespoons tahini
2 tablespoons olive oil
1 tablespoon chopped fresh
    dill weed or 1 teaspoon
    dried dill weed
1 teaspoon ground cumin
1/2 teaspoon salt
1 or 2 cloves garlic,
    coarsely chopped

### Stir in:
1/4 cup chopped fresh parsley

1. Place the eggplant in a dark baking pan. Cover and bake in the solar cooker until tender when tested with a fork, 2 to 3 hours. Cool and drain.

2. In a blender, puree the eggplant with the lemon juice, tahini, olive oil, dill weed, cumin, salt, and garlic until smooth.

3. Stir in the parsley. Scrape into a bowl to serve or store in the fridge.

# CHIPOTLE LENTIL HUMMUS

MAKES about 2 cups  |  COOK 2 to 3 hours  |  **GLUTEN FREE, VEGAN**

*Lentils are faster to cook and have more protein than beans, and they make a great base for this flavorful hummus. Slather it on tortillas as the basis of tostadas or enjoy it on crackers. Adjust the amount of chipotle pepper or chipotle chili powder to suit your taste; this is moderately spicy.*

**Into the cooker:**

1 cup dried red lentils

2 cups water

**Into the blender:**

1/4 cup tahini

1/4 cup olive oil

2 tablespoons tomato paste

1 tablespoon chipotle peppers in adobo sauce, seeds removed, or 1 teaspoon chipotle chili powder

1/2 teaspoon salt

1/2 teaspoon honey

1. Place the lentils and water in a dark baking pan and stir well. Cover and bake in the solar cooker until the lentils are mushy, 2 to 3 hours. Allow to cool.

2. In a blender, puree the lentils and their cooking liquid with the tahini, olive oil, tomato paste, chipotles, salt, and honey until smooth. Scrape into a bowl to serve or store in the fridge.

# RED PEPPER OR SWEET POTATO HUMMUS

MAKES about 3 cups  |  COOK 1 to 2 hours  |  **GLUTEN FREE, VEGAN**

*The red pepper or sweet potato gives this hummus a slightly sweeter taste than regular hummus and also adds nutrition.*

**Into the cooker:**

1 medium orange-fleshed
    sweet potato (sometimes
    called a yam), peeled and
    cut into 1/2-inch cubes

*or*

1 red bell pepper, cored,
    seeded, and chopped

**Into the blender:**

15-ounce can garbanzo beans,
    drained after reserving
    1/4 cup liquid

1/4 cup olive oil

1/4 cup tahini

3 tablespoons fresh lemon juice

1/2 teaspoon salt

1 or 2 cloves garlic,
    coarsely chopped

1.  Place the sweet potato or bell pepper in a dark baking pan. Cover and bake in the solar cooker until tender when tested with a fork, 1 to 2 hours. Allow to cool.

2.  In a blender, puree the sweet potato or red pepper with the garbanzo beans and reserved liquid, olive oil, tahini, lemon juice, salt, and garlic until smooth. Scrape into a bowl to serve or store in the fridge.

# BEET AND WHITE BEAN HUMMUS

MAKES about 2 cups | COOK 4 to 6 hours | **GLUTEN FREE, VEGAN**

*The color is startling but the taste on crackers or pita bread is earthy and robust.*

### Into the cooker:

1 medium beet, greens and root
　　trimmed off

### Into the blender:

15-ounce can great northern
　　or white kidney beans,
　　drained and rinsed
2 tablespoons fresh lemon juice
2 tablespoons tahini
2 tablespoons olive oil
1/2 teaspoon salt

1. Place the beet in a dark baking pan. Cover and bake in the solar cooker until tender when tested with a fork, 4 to 6 hours or longer. Allow to cool, and then rub off the peel with a paper towel. Slice large chunks into a blender.

2. In the blender, puree the beets with the beans, lemon juice, tahini, olive oil, and salt until smooth. Scrape into a bowl to serve or store in the fridge.

# CARROT HUMMUS WITH DILL

MAKES about 1-1/2 cups  |  COOK 2 to 3 hours  |  **GLUTEN FREE, VEGAN**

*Carrots are a root vegetable that takes naturally to solar cooking, the absolutely best and easiest method to prepare them. Carrots that have been cut into pieces, as in this recipe, take less time to cook than those left whole. Maybe you didn't know that you can make hummus with carrots. They lend a slight sweetness, making this taste great on rice crackers or rye crackers.*

**Into the cooker:**
6 medium carrots, diced
    (about 3 cups)

**Into the blender:**
1/4 cup olive oil
2 tablespoons tahini
1 teaspoon cumin
1 teaspoon smoked paprika
1 tablespoon chopped fresh
    dill weed or 1 teaspoon
    dried dill weed
1/2 teaspoon salt
1 or 2 cloves garlic,
    coarsely chopped

1. Place the carrots in a dark baking pan. Cover and bake in the solar cooker until tender when tested with a fork, 2 to 3 hours. Allow to cool.

2. In a blender, puree the carrots with the olive oil, tahini, cumin, paprika, dill weed, salt, and garlic until smooth. Scrape into a bowl to serve or store in the fridge.

# ROSEMARY SOCCA

MAKES 4 wedges | COOK 3 to 4 hours | **GLUTEN FREE, VEGAN**

*Socca (SO-kah), also called farinata, is a chickpea pancake. It's full of protein, chewy and flavorful (the rosemary here can be left out or replaced with other herbs you may have on hand), and pairs well with chilled soups and/or just about any of the spreads in this section. You can also use it as a base for pizza toppings (try solar-cooked beets, pine nuts, arugula, and feta), returning it to the solar cooker for a half hour to an hour to warm the toppings and melt any cheese. It's best fresh out of the cooker, so make only as much as you think you'll eat in one sitting. This makes enough for four appetizer servings or two servings as a side with soup or salad.*

1 cup chickpea (garbanzo) flour
1 cup water
2 tablespoons olive oil
1 teaspoon minced fresh rosemary
1/2 teaspoon salt

1. In a large mixing bowl, whisk together the flour, water, olive oil, rosemary, and salt until smooth.

2. Generously oil a dark 9-to-10-inch-round cake pan or roaster. Pour in the batter. Place in the solar cooker and bake uncovered until dry and completely set, 3 to 4 hours.

3. Allow to cool, score into 4 wedges, and use a spatula to remove from the pan.

# ALMOND CHEESE BISCUITS

**MAKES 8 biscuits** | **COOK 3 to 4 hours** | **GLUTEN FREE, VEGETARIAN**

*I like baking with almond flour because it has more protein than wheat flour and more heft, and it avoids the issue of gluten. For the sake of simplicity, I bake these biscuits like brownies. You can also divide the dough into 8 equal portions, roll each into a ball, and place them on a dark oiled baking sheet to cook. They make a tasty accompaniment to chilled soups and are also a great trail food. You can substitute sunflower seeds for the cheddar cheese to cut down on dairy.*

2 cups almond flour
2 teaspoons baking powder
1/2 teaspoon salt
1/2 teaspoon garlic powder
1/4 teaspoon ground black pepper
2 large eggs, beaten
1/4 cup plain yogurt
1/4 cup avocado oil
1/2 cup (2 ounces) grated
    Parmesan cheese
1 cup (4 ounces) shredded
    cheddar cheese or 1/2 cup
    raw sunflower seeds

1. In a large mixing bowl, combine the flour, baking powder, salt, garlic powder, and pepper, and mix well. In a smaller bowl, whisk together the eggs, yogurt, and oil.

2. Add the wet ingredients to the dry and stir until evenly mixed. Fold in the Parmesan and cheddar or sunflower seeds.

3. Oil a dark 7-by-11-inch pan. Scrape the batter into the pan and even out the surface with the moistened back of a large spoon. Place the pan in the solar cooker uncovered and bake until a toothpick inserted into the center comes out clean, 3 to 4 hours.

4. Allow to cool before slicing into bars and removing from the pan with a spatula to serve.

# CORNMEAL CURRANT SCONES

MAKES 8 scones  |  COOK 2 to 3 hours  |  **VEGETARIAN**

*These scones adapted from* Moosewood Restaurant Cooks at Home *are slightly crunchy and slightly sweet. They go well with salads and cold soups, and also make great trail food. You can substitute finely diced dried apricots, dried cranberries, or dried blueberries for the currants.*

4 tablespoons unsalted butter
    (1/2 stick)
2 tablespoons honey
1/2 cup milk or plain unsweetened
    nondairy milk
3/4 cup yellow cornmeal
3/4 cup unbleached white flour
1/4 cup currants
1 teaspoon baking powder
1/4 teaspoon salt

1. Melt the butter and honey in a dark pan placed in the solar cooker for a few minutes. Then mix in the milk.

2. In a large mixing bowl, stir together the cornmeal, flour, currants, baking powder, and salt. Then add the liquid ingredients to the dry ingredients and stir until the mixture forms a large ball.

3. On a floured board, roll the dough ball into an 8-inch circle about 1/2 inch thick. Slice the circle into eighths. Separate the eight wedges and place them on a dark oiled baking sheet. Bake uncovered in the solar cooker until golden, 2 to 3 hours.

# CRUSTY GREEN OLIVE AND CHEDDAR BREAD

MAKES 1 small round loaf | COOK 2 to 3 hours | **VEGETARIAN**

*I avoided making yeast breads for years because all the kneading put me right off. This bread, which slices beautifully and pairs well with dips and spreads, doesn't require any kneading. Make the dough in the evening and let it rise overnight. Then get it into the solar cooker by 10 AM to scoop the hours of strongest sunlight. I like baking this in a Dutch oven with a clear glass cover so I can watch the progress as it browns.*

2-1/3 cups all-purpose flour

1-1/2 teaspoons active dry yeast

1 teaspoon salt

10 medium pitted green olives, halved lengthwise and thinly sliced

1 cup (4 ounces) shredded sharp cheddar cheese

1 cup + 2 tablespoons warm water

1. In a large mixing bowl, stir together the flour, yeast, and salt. Then stir in the olives and cheese. Finally, stir in the warm water. The dough will be sticky. Gently shape it into a ball as best you can and cover tightly with plastic wrap or aluminum foil. Let it rise at room temperature for 12 to 18 hours.

2. Liberally oil the sides of a dark round baking pan or Dutch oven and cut a piece of waxed or parchment paper to place in the bottom. Use a spatula to turn the dough, which will have doubled in size, into the prepared pan and pat into a loaf. Cover and bake for 2 to 3 hours in the solar cooker, until the loaf sounds hollow when tapped.

3. Carefully remove the bread from the pan, peel the paper off the bottom, and allow to cool before slicing.

# CHILI CHEESE CORNBREAD

MAKES 9 squares | COOK 3 to 4 hours | **GLUTEN FREE, VEGETARIAN**

*This souped-up version of cornbread, based on a recipe from my grandmother, is chewy and moist. Double the butter and cheese if you dare (as my grandma did) for pure comfort food.*

2 tablespoons salted butter
   (1/4 stick)
1 cup yellow cornmeal
1 teaspoon baking powder
1/2 teaspoon salt
2 eggs
3/4 cup plain yogurt
   or sour cream
1 cup fresh or frozen corn kernels
4-ounce can diced green chilis,
   drained and rinsed
1 cup (4 ounces) shredded
   cheddar cheese

1. Melt the butter in a dark 8-or 9-inch-square baking pan placed in the solar cooker for a few minutes. Swirl to coat the pan.

2. In a large mixing bowl, stir together the cornmeal, baking powder, and salt. In a smaller mixing bowl, whisk the eggs, then whisk in the yogurt or sour cream and then the melted butter from the baking pan. Add the liquid ingredients to the dry ingredients. Stir in the corn, chilis, and cheese. Scrape into the buttered baking pan.

3. Place the pan in the solar cooker uncovered and bake until a toothpick inserted into the center comes out clean, 3 to 4 hours. Allow to cool before cutting into squares.

# PUMPKIN-GINGER BREAD

MAKES 1 loaf  |  COOK 2 to 3 hours  |  **VEGAN**

*Pumpkin pie spices and crystallized ginger give a nice zing to this chewy bread. The batter is dark and holds the heat, speeding up the cooking.*

1 cup canned pumpkin

1/4 cup maple syrup

2 tablespoons avocado oil

1 teaspoon vanilla extract

1-3/4 cups unbleached
  all-purpose flour

1/2 cup coconut sugar, xylitol,
  or granulated monkfruit
  sweetener

2 teaspoons baking powder

2 teaspoons ground cinnamon

1/2 teaspoon ground nutmeg

1/2 teaspoon ground allspice

1/2 teaspoon salt

1/4 teaspoon ground cloves

1/4 cup finely chopped
  crystallized ginger

1. In a medium bowl, whisk together the pumpkin, maple syrup, oil, and vanilla extract. In a separate large bowl, combine the flour, granulated sweetener, baking powder, cinnamon, nutmeg, allspice, salt, and cloves, and mix well. Add the wet ingredients to the dry ingredients and mix until smooth before adding the ginger. Stir well.

2. Oil a dark 9-by-5-by-3-inch loaf pan. Scrape the batter into the loaf pan and even out the surface. Place the pan in the solar cooker uncovered and bake until a toothpick inserted into the center comes out clean, 2 to 3 hours.

3. Run a knife around the edge of the pan. Then place a cookie sheet over the pan and invert the pan, letting the bread fall out. Allow the bread to cool before slicing.

# APPLESAUCE OAT BREAD

MAKES 1 loaf  |  COOK 2 to 3 hours  |  **GLUTEN FREE, VEGETARIAN**

*This is a sweet bread with a chewy texture that makes a good snack, trail food, or accompaniment to a chilled soup. To mash the banana, I cut it into little pieces in a bowl and use a potato masher. Use prepared applesauce or make your own (see Applesauce as Nature Intended in Basics and Bonus Recipes).*

1 ripe banana

2 eggs

1 cup applesauce

1/3 cup maple syrup

2 teaspoons ground cinnamon

1 teaspoon vanilla extract

1/4 teaspoon salt

3 cups quick rolled oats

1 cup walnut pieces

1/2 cup chopped dried cranberries

1. In a large mixing bowl, mash the banana, then whisk in the eggs, then the applesauce, maple syrup, cinnamon, vanilla extract, and salt. Stir in the oats, walnut pieces, and cranberries until well combined.

2. Oil a dark 9-by-5-by-3-inch loaf pan. Scrape the batter into the loaf pan and even out the surface. Place the pan in the solar cooker uncovered and bake until a toothpick inserted into the center comes out clean, 2 to 3 hours.

3. Run a knife around the edge of the pan. Then place a cookie sheet over the pan and invert the pan, letting the bread fall out. Allow the bread to cool before slicing.

# Chilled Veggie Soups

*Chipotle Red Pepper Bisque*

# BEET AND CUCUMBER SOUP

SERVES 4  |  COOK 4 to 6 hours or all day  |  **GLUTEN FREE, VEGAN**

*Purple soup! The beets lend an earthy sweetness and the horseradish gives it a kick.
The ume plum vinegar gives it just enough saltiness. Pair this soup with Crustless
Crab Quiche or Sesame Salmon and Orange Salad for a nourishing summer meal.*

### Into the cooker:

2 medium beets, peeled and
    coarsely chopped
1 yellow onion, diced
1-1/2 cups water

### For the finish:

2 large cucumbers, peeled, seeded,
    and coarsely chopped
2 tablespoons olive oil
1 tablespoon prepared horseradish
1-1/2 tablespoons ume plum vinegar

chopped fresh dill weed
    for garnish

1. Place the beets, onion, and
   water in a dark baking pan.
   Cover and bake in the solar
   cooker until the beets are tender
   when tested with a fork,
   4 to 6 hours or longer.

2. Let the vegetables cool and
   then transfer with their liquid
   to a blender or food processer,
   or use a handheld immersion
   blender. Add the cucumber, oil,
   horseradish, and vinegar, and
   blend until smooth.

3. Chill before serving.
   Garnish with fresh dill weed.

*WHY ADD WATER WHEN COOKING VEGGIES? You may notice that almost all the
recipes for veggie soups in this book have you add water to the pan you're cooking
the veggies in. Although the water slows down cooking slightly and isn't strictly
necessary for baking veggies, I like the way it mellows the veggie flavors. Plus you
can truly set it and forget it, leaving the veggies in the cooker all day long.*

# CELERY ROOT SOUP

**SERVES 4  |  COOK 3 to 4 hours or all day  |  GLUTEN FREE, VEGAN**

*Celery root (celeriac) makes a most refreshing chilled summer soup, made creamy with the inclusion of a potato, and a tart apple to lift the flavor. Pairs well with Miso Baked Salmon and Sour Cream Dill Potato Salad.*

### Into the cooker:

1-1/4 pounds celery root, peeled and diced
1 yellow onion, diced
1 large or 2 small Yukon Gold potatoes, peeled and diced
1 medium tart apple, such as Granny Smith, peeled, cored, and diced
1 cup water

### For the finish:

2 cups water
1/4 cup olive oil
1 tablespoon apple cider vinegar
1 teaspoon celery salt
freshly ground black pepper to taste

chopped fresh chives or tarragon, and pecan pieces for garnish

1. Place the celery root, onion, potatoes, apple, and water in a dark baking pan. Cover and bake in the solar cooker until the onion is tender when tested with a fork, 3 to 4 hours or longer.

2. Let the vegetables cool and then transfer with their liquid to a blender or food processer, or use a handheld immersion blender. Add the 2 cups of water, olive oil, vinegar, salt, and pepper, and blend until smooth.

3. Chill before serving. Garnish with chives or tarragon and pecan pieces.

# CHIPOTLE RED PEPPER BISQUE

**SERVES 4 to 6  |  COOK 3 to 4 hours or all day  |  GLUTEN FREE, VEGAN**

*A bisque is a creamy soup of pureed vegetables. This one is crunchy as much as creamy. The bell peppers give it sweetness and the chipotle gives it a kick. Add more or less chipotle to suit your taste. It's nice accompanied with a tortilla spread with refried beans and sprinkled with cheese and then placed in the solar cooker until the cheese melts.*

### Into the cooker:

4 red bell peppers, cored, seeded, and chopped

2 medium Yukon Gold potatoes, peeled and diced

1 yellow onion, diced

1 stalk celery, diced

1 large carrot, diced

1 cup water

### For the finish:

1 cup water

1/4 cup olive oil

2 tablespoons apple cider vinegar

1 teaspoon salt

1/4 to 1/2 teaspoon chipotle chili powder, to taste

chopped fresh parsley and pine nuts for garnish

1. Place the peppers, potatoes, onion, celery, carrot, and water in a dark baking pan. Cover and bake in the solar cooker until the onion is tender when tested with a fork, 3 to 4 hours or longer.

2. Let the vegetables cool and then transfer with their liquid to a blender or food processer, or use a handheld immersion blender. Add the 1 cup water, olive oil, vinegar, salt, and chipotle pepper, and puree.

3. Chill before serving. Garnish with parsley and pine nuts.

# SHAKSHUKA TOMATO SOUP

SERVES 4  |  COOK 3 to 4 hours or all day  |  **GLUTEN FREE, VEGAN**

*Although I do like making gazpacho (raw veggie soup) as the ripe tomatoes start rolling in toward summer's end, roasting the tomatoes in the solar cooker deepens their flavor. This soup borrows spices from the North African comfort food with the name that's fun to say. Pairs well with Almond Cheese Biscuits or Chili Cheese Cornbread and a green salad for a light dinner.*

### Into the cooker:

4 large beefsteak tomatoes, skin on, cored, seeded, and chopped

2 red bell peppers, cored, seeded, and chopped

1 yellow onion, diced

2–3 cloves garlic, chopped

1 cup water

### For the finish:

1/4 cup olive oil

2 tablespoons red wine vinegar

1 teaspoon salt

1 teaspoon harissa (Tunisian hot chili pepper paste)

1/2 teaspoon ground cumin

1/2 teaspoon ground turmeric

1/2 teaspoon smoked paprika

freshly ground black pepper to taste

chopped fresh mint or dill weed, crumbled feta (dairy or nondairy), sliced pitted kalamata olives for garnish

1. Place the tomatoes, peppers, onion, garlic, and water in a dark baking pan. Cover and bake in the solar cooker until the onion is tender when tested with a fork, 3 to 4 hours or longer.

2. Let the vegetables cool and then transfer with their liquid to a blender or food processer, or use a handheld immersion blender. Add the olive oil, vinegar, salt, harissa, cumin, turmeric, paprika, and pepper, and pulse just briefly.

3. Chill before serving. Garnish with mint or dill weed, feta, and olives.

# TOMATO AND ZUCCHINI BISQUE

SERVES 4 | COOK 3 to 4 hours or all day | **GLUTEN FREE, VEGAN**

*A refreshing and flavorful late-summer dish for when you're scrambling to keep up with ripening tomatoes and zucchini. This can stay in the cooker all day long and only gets better. Accompany it with Almond Cheese Biscuits or Chili Cheese Cornbread and a green salad for a light, healthy dinner.*

**Into the cooker:**

4 large beefsteak tomatoes, skin on, cored, seeded, and chopped
1 large zucchini, chopped
1 yellow onion, diced
1 cup water

**For the finish:**

3/4 cup water
1/4 cup tomato paste
2 tablespoons red wine
2 tablespoons olive oil
2 tablespoons apple cider vinegar
1 teaspoon salt
1/2 teaspoon coconut sugar
1/4 teaspoon ground black pepper

chopped fresh oregano or basil, and pine nuts for garnish

1. Place the tomatoes, zucchini, onion, and water in a dark baking pan. Cover and bake in the solar cooker until the onion is tender when tested with a fork, 3 to 4 hours or longer.

2. Let the vegetables cool and then transfer with their liquid to a blender or food processor, or use a handheld immersion blender. Add the 3/4 cup water, tomato paste, red wine, olive oil, vinegar, salt, sugar, and pepper, and puree.

3. Chill before serving. Garnish with fresh oregano or basil and pine nuts.

# ZUCCHINI AND FRESH BASIL SOUP

SERVES 4  |  COOK 1 to 2 hours  |  **VEGAN**

*This soup is light and refreshing, plus it uses three zucchinis in one fell swoop, a coup for any gardener drowning in zucchini. Because zucchinis are mostly water, the recipe uses bread to add a little body. If you don't have bread on hand, you can substitute an equal volume of crackers. Just soak them in the 2 cups of water beforehand. Pairs well with Sesame-Ginger Lentil and Quinoa Salad.*

**Into the cooker:**
3 large zucchini, diced

**For the finish:**
2 cups water
1 thick bread slice, torn into pieces
1/4 cup chopped fresh basil
1/4 cup chopped fresh parsley
1/4 cup olive oil
1/4 cup fresh lemon juice
1 teaspoon maple syrup
1 teaspoon salt
freshly ground black pepper
    to taste

pine nuts for garnish

1. Place the zucchini in a dark baking pan. Cover and bake in the solar cooker until tender when tested with a fork, 1 to 2 hours.

2. Let the zucchini cool and then transfer with its liquid to a blender or food processer. Add the water, bread, basil, parsley, olive oil, lemon juice, salt, and pepper, and puree.

3. Chill before serving. Garnish with pine nuts.

# ZUCCHINI AND CARROT SOUP

SERVES 4  |  COOK 3 to 4 hours or all day  |  **GLUTEN FREE, VEGAN**

*Here's another way to use all those zucchini. This can stay in the cooker all day long and only gets better. Pairs well with Almond Cheese Biscuits or Chili Cheese Cornbread for a light summer lunch.*

**Into the cooker:**

2 large zucchini, diced

3 medium carrots, diced

1 yellow onion, diced

4 cloves garlic, minced

1 cup water

**For the finish:**

2 cups water

1/4 cup olive oil

2 tablespoons apple cider vinegar

1 teaspoon salt

coarsely chopped oil-marinated
    sun-dried tomatoes for garnish

1. Place the zucchini, carrots, onion, garlic, and water in a dark baking pan. Cover and bake in the solar cooker until the onion is tender when tested with a fork, 3 to 4 hours or longer.

2. Let the vegetables cool and then transfer with their liquid to a blender or food processer, or use a handheld immersion blender. Add the 2 cups water, olive oil, vinegar, and salt, and puree.

3. Chill before serving. Garnish with chopped sun-dried tomatoes.

# CREAMY CARROT SOUP WITH DILL

SERVES 4  |  COOK 3 to 4 hours or all day  |  **GLUTEN FREE, VEGETARIAN OR VEGAN**

*Carrots are among the root vegetables that love to be cooked slowly with sunshine. I have to admit that I don't try to grow carrots in my garden since they're so plentiful and affordable at the market. This soup pairs well with Almond Cheese Biscuits or Chili Cheese Cornbread and a green salad.*

**Into the cooker:**

6 medium carrots, diced

1 medium red or yellow potato, peeled and diced

2 stalks celery, diced

1 yellow onion, diced

1 cup water

**For the finish:**

1-1/2 cups water

1 cup half and half or plain unsweetened nondairy milk

1/4 cup olive oil

2 tablespoons apple cider vinegar

1 tablespoon chopped fresh dill weed or 1 teaspoon dried dill weed

1 teaspoon salt

pecan pieces for garnish

1. Place the carrots, potato, celery, onion, and water in a dark baking pan. Cover and bake in the solar cooker until the carrots and potato are tender when tested with a fork, 3 to 4 hours or longer.

2. Let the vegetables cool and then transfer with their liquid to a blender or food processer, or use a handheld immersion blender. Add the 1-1/2 cups water, half and half or milk, olive oil, vinegar, dill weed, and salt, and puree.

3. Chill before serving. Garnish with pecan pieces.

# CURRIED CARROT AND APPLE SOUP

SERVES 4  |  COOK 3 to 4 hours or all day  |  **GLUTEN FREE, VEGAN**

*This soup is slightly sweet and pairs well with Applesauce Oat Bread.*

### Into the cooker:

4 medium carrots, diced

1 yellow onion, diced

2 medium apples, peeled, cored,
    and diced

1 cup apple juice

### For the finish:

1 cup water

14-ounce can coconut milk
    (1-1/2 cups)

1 teaspoon curry powder

1/2 teaspoon turmeric

1/2 teaspoon salt

thinly sliced fresh basil for garnish

1. Place the carrots, onion, apples, and apple juice in a dark baking pan. Cover and bake in the solar cooker until the carrots are tender when tested with a fork, 3 to 4 hours or longer.

2. Let the vegetables cool and then transfer with their liquid to a blender or food processer, or use a handheld immersion blender. Add the water, coconut milk, curry powder, turmeric, and salt, and blend. This soup tastes best if a little chunky in consistency.

3. Chill before serving. Garnish with sliced basil.

# THAI CARROT AND SWEET POTATO SOUP

SERVES 4 to 6  |  COOK 3 to 4 hours or all day  |  **GLUTEN FREE, VEGAN**

*This soup is slightly sweet, with a little bit of a kick from the red curry paste, and pairs well with Applesauce Oat Bread. Note that it calls for raw almond butter. This type of almond butter is runnier than butters made with roasted almonds. If you have only roasted almond butter on hand, just add a little more water.*

### Into the cooker:

1 large or 2 medium orange-fleshed
    sweet potatoes (sometimes
    called yams), peeled and diced
4 medium carrots, diced
1 large yellow onion, diced
2 cloves garlic, minced
1 cup water

### For the finish:

3 cups water, divided
1/2 cup raw almond butter
1/4 cup fresh lime juice
3 tablespoons red curry paste
2 tablespoons maple syrup
1 teaspoon finely grated fresh
    ginger
1 teaspoon salt
dash ground black pepper
    and cayenne pepper

chopped fresh cilantro and finely
    chopped almonds or peanuts
    for garnish

1. Place the sweet potatoes, carrots, onion, garlic, and water in a dark baking pan. Cover and bake in the solar cooker until the carrots are tender when tested with a fork, 3 to 4 hours or longer.

2. Let the vegetables cool and then transfer with their liquid to a blender or food processer, or use a handheld immersion blender. In a small bowl, whisk 1/2 cup water with the almond butter, lime juice, and red curry paste. Add the almond butter mixture to the blender or food processor along with the maple syrup, ginger, salt, pepper, and another 2 cups water, and blend until smooth. Add more water to reach desired consistency.

3. Chill before serving. Garnish with cilantro and chopped almonds or peanuts.

# CURRIED BUTTERNUT SQUASH SOUP

SERVES 4 | COOK 2 to 3 hours | **GLUTEN FREE, VEGAN**

*This soup surprises people with its refreshing taste, achieved with fresh ginger and lime juice. I love how easy it is to cook the squash in the solar cooker. No peeling required! Adjust the amount of water to suit your taste. Good served with Applesauce Oat Bread.*

**Into the cooker:**

1 medium butternut squash (about 2 pounds), topped and cut in half lengthwise

**For the finish:**

2 cups water

14-ounce can coconut milk (1-1/2 cups)

1/4 cup fresh lime juice

2 tablespoons finely grated fresh ginger

1 tablespoon curry powder

1 teaspoon salt

chopped fresh basil and cashews for garnish

1. Place the squash cut side down in a dark baking pan. Cover and bake in the solar cooker until tender when tested with a fork, 2 to 3 hours. Cool, then scoop out and discard the seeds, and scoop the butternut squash out of its skin.

2. In a blender, or using a handheld immersion blender, process the squash along with the water, coconut milk, lime juice, ginger, curry powder, and salt until smooth. Add more water if needed to reach desired consistency.

3. Chill before serving. Garnish with chopped fresh basil and cashews.

# BUTTERNUT SQUASH AND PEAR SOUP

SERVES 4  |  COOK 3 to 4 hours or all day  |  **GLUTEN FREE, VEGAN**

*The flavors of winter squash and fresh pears blend amazingly well in this soup. Good served with Applesauce Oat Bread.*

### Into the cooker:

1 medium butternut squash
    (about 2 pounds), peeled,
    seeded, and diced
1 yellow onion, diced
1 stalk celery, chopped
1 cup water

### For the finish:

3 ripe Bartlett pears,
    cored and chopped
2 cups water
1 cup apple cider
    (not apple cider vinegar)
1 teaspoon finely grated
    fresh ginger
1/2 teaspoon salt

pecan pieces for garnish

1. Place the squash, onion, celery, and water in a dark baking pan. Cover and bake in the solar cooker until the onion is tender when tested with a fork, 3 to 4 hours or longer.

2. Let the vegetables cool and then transfer with their liquid to a blender or food processer, or use a handheld immersion blender. Add the pears, 2 cups water, cider, ginger, and salt, and blend until smooth.

3. Chill before serving. Garnish with pecan pieces.

# CREAMY CAULIFLOWER SOUP WITH THYME

SERVES 4  |  COOK 3 to 4 hours or all day  |  **GLUTEN FREE, VEGETARIAN**

*The day was forecast to be partly cloudy, and as I eyed the sky at 11 AM and tried to decide whether to just go with the indoor oven, I remembered the way cooking cauliflower makes the house smell. Cloudy sky or not, I decided to go with the outdoors. The clouds did eventually disperse, and the garden smelled like cooking cauliflower, to my nose a far more welcome aroma than the smoke from a charcoal grill. This rich and creamy soup makes a nice dinner for a hot day served with Almond Cheddar Biscuits and a green salad.*

**Into the cooker:**

1 head cauliflower, cut into florets
1 small red potato, peeled and diced
1 yellow onion, diced
1 clove garlic, minced
1 cup water

**For the finish:**

1 cup water
1 cup half and half or plain
  unsweetened nondairy milk
1/4 cup olive oil
1 tablespoon apple cider vinegar
1 teaspoon salt
1/4 cup grated Parmesan
1 tablespoon chopped fresh thyme
  or 1 teaspoon dried thyme

chopped hazelnuts for garnish

1. Place the cauliflower, potato, onion, garlic, and water in a dark baking pan. Cover and bake in the solar cooker until the potato and cauliflower are tender when tested with a fork, 3 to 4 hours or longer.

2. Let the vegetables cool and then transfer with their liquid to a blender or food processer, or use a handheld immersion blender. Add 1 cup water, half and half or milk, olive oil, vinegar, and salt, and puree. Stir in the grated Parmesan and thyme. Add more water if needed to reach desired consistency.

3. Chill before serving. Garnish with hazelnuts.

# BROCCOLI AND CARROT BISQUE

**SERVES 6** | COOK 3 to 4 hours or all day | **GLUTEN FREE, VEGAN**

*This is one of those looks-and-smells-bad-but tastes-good deals. Honestly, you just have to trust me on this! The recipe was inspired by one in the delightful vegan cookbook* Isa Does It *by Isa Chandra Moskowitz. It's a good use for solar-cooked broccoli, which loses its bright green color and does not look or smell appetizing. You can always substitute cauliflower for broccoli. Goes nicely with Rosemary Socca.*

### Into the cooker:

4 cups coarsely chopped broccoli, stalks and florets

2 medium carrots, diced

1 yellow onion, diced

2 cloves garlic, minced

2 cups water

### For the finish:

1 cup raw cashews, whole or pieces, soaked for at least 2 hours in enough water to cover

2 cups water

3 tablespoons mellow white miso

2 tablespoons nutritional yeast flakes

2 tablespoons fresh lemon juice

1 tablespoon apple cider vinegar

1 teaspoon salt

diced red onion, red pepper flakes, or smoked paprika for garnish

1. Place the broccoli, carrots, onion, garlic, and water in a dark baking pan. Cover and bake in the solar cooker until the carrots and broccoli are tender when tested with a fork, 3 to 4 hours or longer.

2. Let the vegetables cool and then transfer with their liquid to a blender or food processer, or use a handheld immersion blender. Puree so that tiny bits of broccoli and carrot are visible.

3. Drain the cashews and place them in a blender with 2 cups water and the miso, nutritional yeast, lemon juice, vinegar, and salt. Blend until smooth and add to the broccoli puree. Stir well to combine.

4. Chill before serving. Garnish with red onion, red pepper flakes, or smoked paprika.

# Substantial Salads

CONTINUED ON NEXT PAGE

*Black Lentil Salad with Smoked Trout and Red Peppers*

# RAINBOW CORN SLAW

**SERVES 6  |  COOK 1 to 2 hours  |  GLUTEN FREE, VEGETARIAN OR VEGAN**

*This cool, crunchy, and colorful coleslaw is a summertime staple at my house. Corn on the cob cooked with sunshine tastes much fresher than boiled or microwaved. You can cut the corn off the cob right into a large salad bowl. Brace one end on the bottom of the bowl and slice down from the top with a sharp kitchen knife, turning the cob to expose each uncut surface in turn. Goes well with Mexican food or Miso Baked Salmon.*

### Into the cooker:
3 medium ears of yellow corn, shucked and trimmed (for about 2 cups of kernels)

### For the salad:
1-1/2 cups shredded green cabbage
1-1/2 cups shredded purple cabbage
2 medium carrots, grated
1 small red bell pepper, finely chopped
1/3 cup chopped fresh cilantro
1/3 cup chopped fresh mint
1 tablespoon minced red onion

### For the dressing:
3 tablespoons mayonnaise, regular or vegan
1 tablespoon fresh lemon juice
2 teaspoons Dijon mustard
1/4 teaspoon salt
1/8 to 1/4 teaspoon red chili pepper flakes
1 clove garlic, pressed

1. Place the ears of corn in a dark baking pan. Cover and cook in the solar cooker until steaming, 1 to 2 hours. Allow to cool.

2. Cut the kernels from the cobs into a large salad bowl. Add the cabbage, carrots, bell pepper, cilantro, mint, and onion.

3. Whisk together the mayonnaise, lemon juice, mustard, salt, pepper flakes, and garlic. Pour over the salad and toss gently to combine.

# CORN AND BLUEBERRY SALAD

SERVES 4  |  COOK 1 to 2 hours  |  **GLUTEN FREE, VEGAN**

*This salad dazzles the eyes and the taste buds, and a little goes a long way. The secret is to use blueberries that are perfectly crisp and sweet. Makes a beautiful side with Miso Baked Salmon and Sour Cream Dill Potato Salad.*

**Into the cooker:**

2 medium ears of yellow corn, shucked and trimmed (for about 1-1/2 cups of kernels)

**For the salad and dressing:**

1-1/2 cups fresh blueberries

1/3 cup chopped red bell pepper

2 tablespoons snipped fresh chives

2 tablespoons thinly sliced fresh basil

1 tablespoon honey or maple syrup

1 tablespoon fresh lemon juice

1/4 teaspoon salt

1. Place the ears of corn in a dark baking pan. Cover and cook in the solar cooker until steaming, 1 to 2 hours. Allow to cool.

2. Cut the kernels from the cobs into a salad bowl. Add the blueberries, bell pepper, chives, basil, honey or maple syrup, lemon juice, and salt. Toss gently to combine.

# BEET AND BLUEBERRY SALAD WITH GORGONZOLA

SERVES 4 | COOK 4 to 6 hours | **GLUTEN FREE, VEGETARIAN**

*I can think of lots of ways to use beets in salads, but this may be the most flavorful combo I've discovered. If you don't have perfectly ripe and crisp blueberries on hand, you can always substitute golden raisins. You can also substitute goat cheese for the Gorgonzola. Pair this with Quinoa Tabouli and/or Sesame Salmon, Orange, and Avocado Salad.*

### Into the cooker:
4 medium beets, greens and roots trimmed off

### For the dressing:
3 tablespoons avocado oil
3 tablespoons balsamic vinegar
1 tablespoon honey or maple syrup
1/8 teaspoon salt

### For the salad:
4 cups salad greens or arugula
1 cup fresh blueberries
1/2 cup coarsely chopped almonds or walnuts
1/2 cup crumbled Gorgonzola cheese

1. Place the beets in a dark baking pan. Cover and bake in the solar cooker until tender when tested with a fork, 4 to 6 hours or longer. Allow to cool and then rub off the peel with a paper towel. Dice the beets.

2. Whisk together the oil, vinegar, honey or maple syrup, and salt.

3. Assemble the salad by first tossing the greens with the vinaigrette, then adding the beets and blueberries and tossing, then adding the nuts and tossing, and last adding the cheese and tossing just enough to mix.

# OAT, BLUEBERRY, AND CUCUMBER SALAD

SERVES 4 to 6 | COOK 1 to 2 hours | **GLUTEN FREE, VEGAN**

*Steel-cut oats aren't just for breakfast. Paired with crisp blueberries and cucumbers, they add just the right amount of chewiness to this fresh-tasting salad. Check the oats at 1 hour and don't leave them in the cooker too long, or they'll get gummy on the bottom. They may come out of the cooker seeming gummy anyway, but once you fluff and cool them down, they'll combine well with the other ingredients. This salad tastes best if devoured immediately.*

**Into the cooker:**

1 cup steel cut oats
1–2/3 cups water

**For the salad:**

1 medium cucumber, peeled, seed-
    ed, and finely diced
2 cups fresh blueberries
1/2 cup shelled pistachios, unsalted
2 tablespoons chopped fresh mint

**For the dressing:**

1/4 cup avocado oil
1/4 cup fresh lime juice
zest from 1 lime
2 tablespoons honey or maple syrup
1/2 teaspoon salt

1. Place the oats and water in a dark baking pan and swish briefly to combine. Cover and bake in the solar cooker until the water has been absorbed and the grain is tender, 1 to 2 hours. Remove from the cooker and fluff with a fork. Allow to cool.

2. In a large serving bowl, combine the cooked oats with the cucumber, blueberries, pistachios, and mint.

3. Whisk together the oil, lime juice, zest, honey or maple syrup, and salt. Pour over the salad and mix gently.

# CURRIED BUCKWHEAT AND GARBANZO SALAD

SERVES 4 to 6  |  COOK 1 hour  |  **GLUTEN FREE, VEGAN**

*Buckwheat is quick to cook but gets mushy if you cook it too long, so check its progress at 30 minutes. Like quinoa, buckwheat is gluten free and high in protein—and awfully bland, so it demands a dressing with a bold flavor. You can use either plain buckwheat groats or kasha, which is roasted buckwheat, in this dish. The roasted version has a stronger flavor, which you may or may not like. I prefer the plain myself. This is a very hearty salad and can be paired with a cold soup to round it out. Note that golden raisins are moderately better for you than regular, as they have more flavonoids, which have antioxidant properties.*

### Into the cooker:
1 cup buckwheat groats, rinsed
1-1/2 cups water

### For the salad:
1 cup golden raisins
1 cup canned garbanzo beans,
    drained and rinsed
1 cup unsalted peanuts
1 cup baby arugula
2 tablespoons chopped chives
    or green onions

### For the dressing:
1/3 cup avocado oil
3 tablespoons apple cider vinegar
1 tablespoon tamari
    (wheat-free soy sauce)
2 teaspoons curry powder
1 teaspoon dry mustard
1/2 teaspoon salt
1/8 teaspoon ground black pepper

1. Place the buckwheat and water in a dark baking pan and swish briefly to combine. Cover and bake in the solar cooker until the water has been absorbed, 1 hour or less. Remove from the cooker, fluff well with a fork, and allow to cool.

2. In a large serving bowl, combine the buckwheat with the raisins, garbanzos, peanuts, arugula, and chives or green onions.

3. Whisk together the oil, vinegar, tamari, curry powder, dry mustard, salt, and pepper. Pour over the salad and mix well.

# DILL BROWN RICE SALAD

SERVES 4 | COOK 2 to 3 hours | **GLUTEN FREE, VEGAN**

*I've been making this salad ever since I was just out of college and learning how to cook healthy food for myself. With tofu in the dressing, it's the classic protein pairing of rice and beans. This salad keeps well in the fridge for several days but tastes best if eaten at room temperature. To make a meal out of it, top it with sliced tomatoes, cucumbers, and/or radishes, whatever the garden is currently producing in abundance, and a dash of salty ume plum vinegar.*

**Into the cooker:**

1 cup long grain brown rice, rinsed

1-3/4 cups water

**For the salad:**

1 medium carrot, grated

4 green onions, sliced, or 2 table-
    spoons snipped fresh chives

**For the dressing:**

8 ounces firm tofu (not silken)

1/4 cup water

2 tablespoons olive oil

2 tablespoons apple cider vinegar

1 tablespoon chopped fresh
    dill weed or 1 teaspoon dried
    dill weed

1 teaspoon salt

1. Place the brown rice and water in a dark baking pan and swish briefly to combine. Cover and bake in the solar cooker until all the liquid has been absorbed, 2 to 3 hours. Remove from the cooker, fluff with a fork, and allow to cool.

2. In a large serving bowl, combine the rice with the carrot and green onions or chives.

3. In a blender, puree the tofu, water, oil, vinegar, dill, and salt until smooth. Pour over the rice mixture and gently stir together.

# QUINOA, POMEGRANATE, AND PISTACHIO SALAD

SERVES 4 to 6  |  COOK 1 to 2 hours  |  **GLUTEN FREE, VEGAN**

*This a good use for bland quinoa, which makes this salad really filling. Since I don't have a pomegranate tree, I wait for pomegranate seeds to appear in the market every year so I can make it. The dressing is absolutely addictive.*

### Into the cooker:
1 cup quinoa, rinsed
1-1/2 cups water

### For the salad:
1 cup pomegranate seeds
1 cup roasted and salted
    shelled pistachios
2 tablespoons fresh snipped chives

### For the dressing:
1/4 cup water
1/4 cup tahini
2 tablespoons fresh lemon juice
2 tablespoons coconut aminos
1 tablespoon avocado oil
1/2 teaspoon cumin

1. Place the quinoa and water in a dark baking pan and swish briefly to combine. Cover and bake in the solar cooker until the water has been absorbed, the grain has become transparent, and the spiral-like germ has separated, 1 to 2 hours. Remove from the cooker, fluff with a fork, and allow to cool.

2. In a large serving bowl, combine the quinoa with the pomegranate seeds, pistachios, and chives.

3. Whisk together the water, tahini, lemon juice, coconut aminos, oil, and cumin. Pour over the quinoa mixture and gently stir together.

# QUINOA TABOULI

SERVES 4 to 6 | COOK 1 to 2 hours | **GLUTEN FREE, VEGAN**

*I like substituting quinoa for the bulgur traditionally used in tabouli to get more protein and avoid gluten. English cucumbers don't need to be peeled or seeded; if you use a regular slicing cucumber, be sure to peel and seed it. Add 1/4 cup crumbled feta cheese (dairy or nondairy) for even more protein.*

**Into the cooker:**

1 cup quinoa, rinsed

1-1/2 cups water

**For the salad:**

1 medium tomato, cored, seeded, and finely diced

1 medium English cucumber, finely diced

1/2 cup chopped parsley

2 tablespoons minced fresh mint

**For the dressing:**

3 tablespoons olive oil

3 tablespoons fresh lemon juice

1/2 teaspoon salt

freshly ground black pepper to taste

1 clove garlic, minced

1. Place the quinoa and water in a dark baking pan and swish briefly to combine. Cover and bake in the solar cooker until the water has been absorbed, the grain has become transparent, and the spiral-like germ has separated, 1 to 2 hours. Remove from the cooker, fluff with a fork, and allow to cool.

2. In a large serving bowl, combine the quinoa with the tomato, cucumber, parsley, and mint.

3. Whisk together the oil, lemon juice, salt, pepper, and garlic. Pour over the quinoa mixture and gently stir together.

# CRUNCHY QUINOA AND KALE SALAD

SERVES 4 to 6  |  COOK 1 to 2 hours  |  **GLUTEN FREE, VEGAN**

*This salad is crunchy and sweet. The dressing is so tasty that you'll want to use it on other salads, so the recipe makes extra. Prepare only as much of this salad as you can eat fresh (halve the recipe if necessary), because it doesn't keep well.*

### Into the cooker:
1/2 cup quinoa, rinsed
3/4 cup water

### For the salad:
2 cups very thinly sliced curly green
    kale leaves
1 cup shelled edamame or walnut
    pieces
1 cup quartered and thinly sliced
    radishes
1/4 cup dried currants

### For the dressing:
1/4 cup tahini
1/4 cup white miso
1/4 cup water
2 tablespoons fresh lemon juice
2 tablespoons coconut aminos
1 tablespoon sherry vinegar

1. Place the quinoa and water in a dark baking pan and swish briefly to combine. Cover and bake in the solar cooker until the water has been absorbed, the grain has become transparent, and the spiral-like germ has separated, 1 to 2 hours. Remove from the cooker, fluff with a fork, and allow to cool.

2. In a large serving bowl, combine the quinoa with the kale, edamame or walnuts, radishes, and currants.

3. Whisk together the tahini, miso, water, lemon juice, coconut aminos, and vinegar until emulsified. Add 1/2 cup of the dressing to the salad and toss. Add more to taste.

# BLACK LENTIL SALAD WITH SMOKED TROUT AND RED PEPPERS

SERVES 4  |  COOK 2 to 3 hours  |  **GLUTEN FREE**

*Black lentils, also called beluga lentils, are smaller than other varieties and hold their shape better when cooked. This salad, which is pretty much a meal in itself, keeps well for several days in the fridge if you just hold the avocado until right before you eat it. Recipe adapted from* Adventures in Slow Cooking *by Sarah DiGregorio.*

**Into the cooker:**

1-1/2 cups black (beluga) lentils

3 cups water

**For the salad:**

12-ounce jar roasted red peppers, drained and chopped (about 1 cup)

8 ounces smoked trout filets, flaked

1/4 cup chopped parsley

1/4 cup minced fresh chives

**For the dressing:**

3 tablespoons olive oil

3 tablespoons sherry vinegar

1/2 teaspoon salt

1/4 teaspoon ground black pepper

**To finish:**

1 avocado, diced

2 cups salad greens

fresh lemon juice and salt to taste

1. Place the lentils and water in a dark baking pan and swish briefly to combine. Cover and bake in the solar cooker until the lentils are tender, 2 to 3 hours. Remove from the cooker and allow to cool.

2. In a large serving bowl, combine the lentils with the red peppers, trout, parsley, and chives. Whisk together the oil, vinegar, salt, and pepper. Pour over the lentil mixture and stir gently.

3. Prepare a bed of greens on each plate, add the lentil mixture, then top with the avocado. Sprinkle each salad with lemon juice and additional salt if desired.

# SESAME-GINGER LENTIL AND QUINOA SALAD

SERVES 4 to 6 | COOK 2 to 3 hours | **GLUTEN FREE, VEGAN**

*For this salad, you'll need to cook two dishes at once: the quinoa and the lentils. The combination of lentils and quinoa is filling and nutritious. Pair this with Zucchini and Fresh Basil Soup for a light summer dinner.*

### Into the cooker:

1/2 cup dried green or brown lentils

1 cup water

1/2 cup quinoa, rinsed

3/4 cup water

### For the salad:

1 medium carrot, coarsely grated

1/2 cup thinly sliced and diced
    red cabbage

1/4 cup chopped fresh cilantro
    or parsley

1 tablespoon finely grated
    fresh ginger

### For the dressing:

2 tablespoons ume plum vinegar

2 tablespoons toasted sesame oil

2 tablespoons avocado oil

1. Place the lentils and 1 cup water in a dark baking pan, and place the quinoa and 3/4 cup water in another dark baking pan. Swish briefly to combine. Cover both pans and place in the solar cooker, stacked on top of each other if need be.

2. Bake the quinoa until the water has been absorbed, the grain has become transparent, and the spiral-like germ has separated, 1 to 2 hours. Remove from the cooker, fluff with a fork, and allow to cool. Bake the lentils until the water has been absorbed and the lentils are tender, 2 to 3 hours. Allow to cool.

3. In a large serving bowl, combine the lentils and quinoa with the carrot, cabbage, cilantro, and ginger.

4. Whisk together the vinegar and oils. Pour over the lentil-quinoa mixture and gently stir together.

# GREEN LENTIL SALAD WITH EDAMAME, GRAPES, AND FETA

**SERVES 4 | COOK 2 to 3 hours | GLUTEN FREE, VEGETARIAN OR VEGAN**

*This unlikely combination of ingredients is surprisingly tasty. The salad is best eaten right away and not held over in the fridge. The recipe is adapted from Jackie Freeman's cookbook* Easy Beans. *This pairs nicely with Rosemary Socca and/or Celery Root Soup.*

### Into the cooker:

1 cup dried green lentils

2 cups water

### For the salad:

2 cups arugula

1-1/2 cups halved red
    seedless grapes

1 cup toasted pecan pieces

1/2 cup shelled raw edamame

1/2 cup crumbled feta cheese,
    dairy or nondairy

2 tablespoons torn fresh mint

### For the dressing:

1/4 cup fresh lemon juice

3 tablespoons olive oil

2 tablespoons Dijon mustard

1/4 teaspoon salt

1/8 teaspoon ground black pepper

1. Place the lentils and water in a dark baking pan and swish briefly to combine. Cover and bake in the solar cooker until the lentils are tender, 2 to 3 hours. Allow to cool.

2. In a large serving bowl, combine the lentils with the arugula, grapes, pecan pieces, edamame, feta, and mint.

3. Whisk together the lemon juice, oil, mustard, salt, and pepper. Pour over the lentil mixture and gently stir together.

# SOUR CREAM DILL POTATO SALAD

SERVES 4  |  COOK 2 to 6 hours or all day  |  **GLUTEN FREE, VEGETARIAN**

*I love this potato salad so much I've been known to put it on a bed of arugula and make a whole dinner of it. The skins can be left on the potatoes, which you can cook either whole or cut into bite-sized cubes. Cutting them up before cooking reduces their cooking time. This salad keeps well in the fridge for several days but tastes best if eaten at room temperature.*

**Into the cooker:**

6 medium red potatoes, well
    scrubbed, whole or cubed

**For the dressing:**

1/4 cup sour cream
1/4 cup mayonnaise
1 tablespoon apple cider vinegar
1/4 cup chopped fresh dill weed
    or 1 tablespoon dried dill weed
1/2 teaspoon celery seed
1/4 teaspoon salt
2 green onions, thinly sliced
freshly ground black pepper
    to taste

1.  Place the potatoes, whole or cubed, in a dark baking pan. Cover and bake in the solar cooker until tender when tested with a fork, 2 to 3 hours for cubed potatoes and 4 to 6 hours or longer for whole potatoes.

2.  If you left the potatoes whole, cut them into small cubes while still warm and allow to cool; otherwise, allow the baked cubed potatoes to cool. Place in a large serving bowl.

3.  Whisk together the sour cream, mayonnaise, vinegar, dill weed, celery seed, salt, green onions, and pepper. Fold gently into the potatoes.

# ADOBO POTATO SALAD

SERVES 4 to 6  |  COOK 4 to 6 hours or all day  |  **GLUTEN FREE, VEGETARIAN**

*My favorite recipe in the whole book! Solar-cooked potatoes are creamy, and the chipotle pepper gives this salad just the right amount of kick. It's best if the potatoes are peeled, which I find easier when they've been cooked whole. Before you chop the chipotle pepper, scrape off and reserve any adobo sauce clinging to it so you can use it in the dressing. This salad keeps well in the fridge for several days but tastes best if eaten at room temperature.*

**Into the cooker:**
6 medium red potatoes

**For the salad:**
2 hard-boiled eggs, chopped
1 chipotle from a can of
      chipotle peppers in
      adobo sauce, chopped
1 small red onion, diced
2 tablespoons sweet pickle relish

**For the dressing:**
1/3 cup mayonnaise
1/3 cup yogurt
1 tablespoon Dijon mustard
1 teaspoon adobo sauce
1/2 teaspoon salt

1. Place the whole unpeeled potatoes in a dark baking pan. Cover and bake in the solar cooker until tender when tested with a fork, 4 to 6 hours or longer. Allow to cool.

2. Skin the potatoes and cut into small cubes. Place in a large serving bowl and add the hard-boiled eggs, chipotle pepper, onion, and pickle relish.

3. Whisk together the mayonnaise, yogurt, mustard, adobo sauce, and salt. Fold gently into the potato mixture.

# POTATO SALAD WITH SMOKED SALMON OR TUNA

SERVES 4  |  COOK 2 to 6 hours or all day  |  **GLUTEN FREE**

*This easy dish is a meal in itself if you put it on a bed of salad greens that you've tossed with oil and vinegar and/or serve it with one of the cold soups like Zucchini and Fresh Basil Soup. The skins can be left on the potatoes, which you can cook either whole or cut into bite-sized cubes. Cutting them up before cooking reduces their cooking time. This salad keeps well in the fridge for several days but tastes best if eaten at room temperature.*

### Into the cooker:

6 medium red potatoes,
    well scrubbed, whole or cubed

### For the salad:

1/2 red bell pepper, seeded
    and finely diced
2 tablespoons minced red onion
2 tablespoons capers
2 tablespoons chopped fresh
    parsley or dill weed
8 ounces smoked salmon (not lox)
    or best-quality tuna, drained
    and flaked

### For the dressing:

1/4 cup olive oil
2 tablespoons red wine vinegar
1 tablespoon Dijon mustard
1/2 teaspoon salt

1. Place the potatoes, whole or cubed, in a dark baking pan. Cover and bake in the solar cooker until tender when tested with a fork, 2 to 3 hours for cubed potatoes and 4 to 6 hours or longer for whole potatoes.

2. If you left the potatoes whole, cut them into small cubes while still warm and allow to cool; otherwise, allow the baked cubed potatoes to cool. Place in a large serving bowl. Add the bell pepper, onion, capers, parsley or dill, and salmon or tuna.

3. Whisk together the oil, vinegar, mustard, and salt. Pour over the potato mixture and stir gently to combine.

# CURRIED SWEET POTATO AND RED POTATO SALAD

**SERVES 4  |  COOK 2 to 3 hours  |  GLUTEN FREE, VEGETARIAN OR VEGAN**

*Because sweet potatoes cook more quickly than red potatoes, it's best to cook them separately. You could even cook them consecutively if you start them early enough in the day. Don't overcook the sweet potatoes or they won't hold their shape. This simple potato salad is a great accompaniment to Miso Baked Salmon and a green salad. It keeps well in the fridge for several days but tastes best if eaten at room temperature.*

**Into the cooker:**

4 medium red potatoes, peeled and cut into bite-sized cubes

4 medium orange-fleshed sweet potatoes (sometimes called yams), peeled and cut into bite-sized cubes

**For the dressing:**

1/2 cup mayonnaise, regular or vegan
3 tablespoons mango chutney
2 teaspoons curry powder
3 green onions, thinly sliced

1. Place the red potatoes in a dark baking pan. At the same time, place the sweet potatoes in a dark baking pan. Cover both pans and place in the solar cooker, stacked on top of each other if need be.

2. Bake both kinds of potatoes until tender when tested with a fork, 1 to 2 hours for the sweet potatoes and 2 to 3 hours for the red potatoes. Cool the potatoes and transfer to a large serving bowl.

3. Whisk together the mayonnaise, chutney, curry powder, and green onions. Pour over the potato chunks and toss gently until thoroughly coated.

# SWEET POTATO AND KALE SALAD WITH CRANBERRIES AND PECANS

SERVES 4 | COOK 1 to 2 hours | **GLUTEN FREE, VEGAN**

*I find this tasty recipe useful when kale starts bolting in the garden and I want to use a lot of it. Be sure to check the sweet potatoes after an hour and don't let them overcook, or they won't hold up. The dressing is so good that you might want to double the recipe so you have some on hand for any other salad you put together. This salad is best eaten right away and not refrigerated.*

### Into the cooker:

1 large orange-fleshed sweet potato (sometimes called a yam), peeled and cut into bite-sized chunks

### For the salad:

4 cups thinly sliced kale leaves
1/2 cup chopped cilantro
1/2 cup unsalted dry toasted pecan pieces
1/4 cup dried cranberries

### For the dressing:

2 tablespoons avocado oil
2 tablespoons tahini
2 tablespoons fresh lime juice
1 tablespoon honey or maple syrup
1/4 teaspoon salt
1/4 teaspoon cumin
pinch cayenne pepper

1. Place the sweet potato chunks in a dark baking pan. Cover and bake in the solar cooker until tender when tested with a fork, 1 to 2 hours. Allow to cool.

2. Place the kale in a large salad bowl, and squeeze and massage the leaves with your fingers until the leaves become soft. Add the cilantro, pecan pieces, and cranberries, and toss to combine. Transfer the sweet potato to the salad bowl.

3. Whisk together the oil, tahini, lime juice, honey or maple syrup, salt, cumin, and cayenne. Pour over the salad and toss gently, just enough to mix.

# FIESTA CHICKEN SALAD

**SERVES 4  |  COOK 1 to 2 hours  |  GLUTEN FREE**

*Lots of different salads are quick and simple to make when you keep solar-cooked chicken breasts on hand. This one stands on its own as dinner. The recipe makes plenty of the cilantro–pumpkin seed dressing, which also serves as a tasty dip for tortilla chips.*

**Into the cooker:**

1 pound boneless and skinless
   chicken breasts

**For the dressing:**

1 cup hot water

2/3 cup raw pumpkin seeds (also
   called pepitas)

1/2 cup coarsely chopped fresh
   cilantro

1/4 cup fresh lime juice

2 tablespoons olive or avocado oil

1 tablespoon maple syrup

1 teaspoon ground cumin

1 teaspoon salt

**For the salad:**

4 cups romaine lettuce, torn
   into bite-sized pieces

15-ounce can black beans,
   drained and rinsed

1 large ripe avocado, peeled
   and diced

1 cup corn kernels

1 cup pico de gallo

4-ounce can sliced black olives

4 ounces (1 cup) grated Jack
   and/or cheddar cheese

tortilla chips

1.  Place the chicken breasts in a dark baking pan. Cover and bake in the solar cooker until no longer pink, 1 to 2 hours. Remove, cool, and shred meat.

2.  In a blender, puree the water, pumpkin seeds, cilantro, lime juice, oil, maple syrup, cumin, and salt until smooth. Add more water as necessary so the texture resembles a creamy ranch dressing.

3.  Place a cup of the lettuce on each dinner plate and top with a quarter of the black beans, avocado, corn, pico de gallo, olives, and cheese. Top with the chicken and a few tortilla chips. Drizzle with the dressing.

# CRANBERRY WALDORF CHICKEN SALAD

SERVES 4  |  COOK 1 to 2 hours  |  **GLUTEN FREE**

*I always hate the job of trimming the fat off of chicken thighs, and this recipe gives an excuse to just put the thighs into the cooker straight out of the package and save that greasy task for when they're cooked, when it seems easier. Pair this chicken salad with Rosemary Socca or Crusty Green Olive and Cheddar Bread and a cold soup for dinner. It's also good served in a pita pocket. For a variation, substitute chopped raw cashews or almonds for the walnuts, and diced celery for the cranberries.*

**Into the cooker:**

1 pound boneless and skinless
    chicken thighs

**For the salad:**

1 small apple of a crisp variety,
    cored and diced
1 cup halved seedless grapes
1/2 cup walnut pieces
1/4 cup chopped dried cranberries

**For the dressing:**

1/3 cup mayonnaise
1 tablespoon apple cider vinegar
1/8 teaspoon salt

**For plating:**

Salad leaves

1. Place the chicken thighs in a dark baking pan. Cover and bake in the solar cooker until no longer pink, 1 to 2 hours. Remove, cool, and slice and/or pull the meat into small chunks.

2. In a large serving bowl, combine the chicken with the apple, grapes, walnuts, and cranberries.

3. Whisk together the mayonnaise, vinegar, and salt until smooth. Pour over the chicken mixture and gently stir together.

4. Place a bed of salad leaves on four plates and distribute the chicken salad.

# CHICKEN AND WILD RICE SALAD

SERVES 4 | COOK 2 to 3 hours | **GLUTEN FREE**

*Wild rice cooks beautifully in the solar cooker. This substantial salad is really all you need for dinner.*

### Into the cooker:
1 pound boneless and skinless chicken breasts

1 cup wild rice
1-3/4 cups water

### For the salad:
1 medium carrot, grated
2 celery stalks with leaves, finely diced
1/2 cup chopped dried cranberries
1/4 cup chopped parsley

### For the dressing:
1/4 cup fresh lemon juice
1/4 cup olive oil
2 tablespoons Dijon mustard
1/2 teaspoon salt
1/8 teaspoon ground black pepper

### For plating:
Salad leaves

1. Place the chicken breasts in a dark baking pan. Cover and bake in the solar cooker until no longer pink, 1 to 2 hours. Remove, cool, and slice and/or pull the meat into small chunks.

2. At the same time, place the wild rice and water in a dark baking pan and swish briefly to combine. Cover and bake until the grains have split open and softened, 2 to 3 hours. Remove and cool.

3. In a large serving bowl, combine the chicken with the rice, carrot, celery, cranberries, and parsley.

4. Whisk together the lemon juice, oil, mustard, salt, and pepper until smooth. Pour over the chicken and rice mixture and gently stir together.

5. Place a bed of salad leaves on four plates and distribute the chicken salad.

# CHICKEN ARUGULA SALAD WITH PEARS AND PECANS

SERVES 4  |  COOK 1 to 2 hours  |  **GLUTEN FREE**

*This simple salad is flavorful and filling. It pairs well with Beet and Cucumber Soup and Applesauce Oat Bread. Make extra dressing to use on other salads.*

**Into the cooker:**

1 pound boneless and skinless
    chicken breasts

**For the salad:**

4 cups arugula
2 large ripe Bartlett pears,
    cored and cubed
1 cup raw pecan halves or pieces
2 tablespoons minced
    candied ginger

**For the dressing:**

1/4 cup avocado oil
2 tablespoons fresh lime juice
1 tablespoon honey or maple syrup
1 teaspoon tamari
    (wheat-free soy sauce)
1 teaspoon fish sauce

1.  Place the chicken breasts in a dark baking pan. Cover and bake in the solar cooker until no longer pink, 1 to 2 hours. Remove, cool, and slice and/or pull the meat into small chunks.

2.  Place a bed of arugula on each dinner plate and top with a quarter of the chicken, pear cubes, pecan pieces, and candied ginger.

3.  Whisk together the oil, lime juice, honey or maple syrup, tamari, and fish sauce. Drizzle on the salads.

# THAI CHICKEN SALAD

**SERVES 4 to 6  |  COOK 1 to 2 hours  |  GLUTEN FREE**

*This is a summertime favorite of mine, using the mint and basil that's plentiful in my garden. It takes a while to chop up all the raw ingredients, but the result is refreshing and flavorful. Combine the salad with Cornmeal Currant Scones or Applesauce Oat Bread to make a meal.*

**Into the cooker:**

1 pound boneless and skinless
   chicken breasts

**For the salad:**

3 cups shredded cabbage, green
   and red
2 medium carrots, coarsely grated
1/2 cup chopped fresh cilantro
1/2 cup diced or slivered almonds
2 tablespoons chopped fresh mint
2 tablespoons chopped fresh basil

**For the dressing:**

1/4 cup fresh lime juice
1/4 cup avocado oil
3 tablespoons honey or maple syrup
2 tablespoons fish sauce
1 tablespoon tamari
   (wheat-free soy sauce)
1 tablespoon finely grated
   fresh ginger
1 teaspoon toasted sesame oil

1. Place the chicken breasts in a dark baking pan. Cover and bake in the solar cooker until no longer pink, 1 to 2 hours. Remove, cool, and slice and/or pull into small chunks.

2. In a large salad bowl, combine the chicken with the cabbage, carrots, cilantro, almonds, mint, and basil.

3. Whisk together the lime juice, oil, honey or maple syrup, fish sauce, tamari, ginger, and sesame oil. Pour over the salad and toss well.

# SESAME SALMON, ORANGE, AND AVOCADO SALAD

SERVES 4  |  COOK 1 hour  |  **GLUTEN FREE**

*Salmon pairs well with citrus in this filling salad. You'll want to check it for doneness after the first 30 minutes to make sure you don't overcook it. Serve with Quinoa Tabouli and Celery Root Soup for a complete meal.*

### Into the cooker:
1 pound salmon fillets, rinsed
    and patted dry
1 teaspoon toasted sesame oil

### For the salad:
4 cups salad greens
2 navel oranges, peeled, quartered
    lengthwise, and sliced
1 large ripe avocado, peeled
    and cubed
1/4 cup thinly sliced red onion
    (optional)

### For the dressing:
2 tablespoons toasted sesame oil
2 tablespoons tamari
    (wheat-free soy sauce)
2 tablespoons maple syrup
1 tablespoon apple cider vinegar

### For the finish:
1 tablespoon sesame seeds

1. Rub the salmon with the sesame oil and place skin-side down in a dark baking pan. Cover and bake in the solar cooker until the fish flakes easily with a fork, 30 minutes to 1 hour. Allow to cool.

2. Place a bed of salad greens on each dinner plate and top with a quarter of the salmon, orange, avocado, and (optional) red onion.

3. Whisk together the sesame oil, tamari, maple syrup, and vinegar. Drizzle on the salads and sprinkle them with sesame seeds.

# Bountiful Bowls

*Parmesan Spinach Polenta Bowl*

# BOWL BUILDING BLOCKS

*I love the idea of a complete meal in one big bowl. There's a loose formula:*

**grains** *(like rice, quinoa, farro)*
+
**protein** *(lentils, beans, tofu, hard-boiled eggs, cheese, poultry, meat, seafood)*
+
**starchy vegetables** *(like sweet potatoes, beets, carrots, winter squash)*
+
**nonstarchy vegetables** *(spinach, cabbage, kale, arugula, lettuce, cucumbers, bell peppers, radishes, and such)*
+
**something crunchy** *(nuts, seeds, croutons)*
+
**a yummy sauce**

*It's easy to cook up a batch of one or more of the following bowl building blocks in your solar cooker to have on hand for spontaneous bowl creation, or follow the recipes in this section.*

## RICE

Place 1 cup rinsed rice to 1-3/4 cups water in a dark baking pan and swish briefly to combine. Cover and place in the solar cooker. Bake until all the liquid has been absorbed, 2 to 3 hours. Remove from the cooker, fluff with a fork, and allow to cool.

## QUINOA

Place 1 cup rinsed quinoa to 1-1/2 cups water in a dark baking pan and swish briefly to combine. Cover and place in the solar cooker. Bake until the water has been absorbed, the grain has become transparent, and the spiral-like germ has separated, 1 to 2 hours. Remove from the cooker, fluff with a fork, and allow to cool.

## FARRO

Place 1 cup pearled or hulled farro to 1-3/4 cups water in a dark baking pan and swish briefly to combine. Cover and place in the solar cooker. Bake until the grain is tender and the water has been absorbed, 2 to 3 hours. Remove from the cooker, fluff with a fork, and allow to cool.

## LENTILS

Place 1 cup lentils to 2 cups water in a dark baking pan and swish briefly to combine. Cover and place in the solar cooker. Bake the lentils until the water has been absorbed and the lentils are tender but not mushy, 2 to 3 hours. Allow to cool.

## CHICKEN

Place boneless and skinless chicken breasts or thighs in a dark baking pan. Cover and place in the solar cooker. Bake until no longer pink, 1 to 2 hours. Remove, cool, and slice and/or pull into small chunks. Save the liquid to use as a soup base or to cook grains in.

## SHRIMP

Place uncooked jumbo shrimp, deveined and peeled or unpeeled, rinsed and patted dry, in a dark baking pan. Cover and place in the solar cooker. Bake until pink and opaque, 1 hour or so. Do not overcook. Allow to cool, and peel if it was unpeeled.

## SALMON

Place salmon fillets, rinsed and patted dry, skin-side down in a dark baking pan. Cover and place in the solar cooker. Bake until the fish flakes easily with a fork, 1 to 2 hours. Do not overcook.

## SWEET POTATOES

Peel and cut into 1/2-inch cubes. Place in a dark baking pan, cover, and put in the solar cooker. Bake until just barely tender when tested with a fork, 1 to 2 hours. Allow to cool.

## BEETS

Cook whole and unpeeled, or peeled and cut into 1/2-inch cubes. Place in a dark baking pan, cover, and put in the solar cooker. Bake until tender when tested with a fork, 4 to 6 hours or longer. Allow to cool, and then if whole, rub off the peel with a paper towel.

# PARMESAN SPINACH POLENTA BOWL

MAKES 4 | COOK 4 to 5 hours | **GLUTEN FREE, VEGETARIAN**

*I love this bowl because it's so easy and satisfying. Polenta (yellow corn grits) turns out beautifully creamy when left undisturbed in the solar cooker for 4 to 5 hours. No tending or stirring needed! Fresh out of the cooker, it's hot enough to wilt spinach and melt cheese that you stir in, so time it to come out of the cooker just before dinner is served. Top it with a mixture of sweet cherry tomatoes and black beans for summertime comfort food. Add a side of tortilla chips for some crunch.*

**Into the cooker:**

1 cup polenta

4 cups water

2 tablespoons butter,
    cut into little bits

1 teaspoon salt

**For the finish:**

1 cup grated Parmesan cheese

3 cups firmly packed baby spinach

**For the bowls:**

15-ounce can black beans,
    drained and rinsed

2 cups halved cherry tomatoes

2 tablespoons olive oil

2 tablespoons balsamic vinegar

2 tablespoons finely minced
    fresh basil

1/2 teaspoon salt

1. Place the polenta, water, butter, and salt in a dark baking pan and stir well. Cover and bake in the solar cooker until thick and tender, 4 to 5 hours. Remove from the cooker and immediately fold in the Parmesan cheese and then the spinach.

2. In a medium bowl, toss the black beans and cherry tomatoes with the oil, vinegar, basil, and salt.

3. Assemble the bowls by putting 1/4 of the polenta in each bowl and evenly distributing the beans and cherry tomatoes.

# GLORY BOWL

MAKES 4  |  COOK 4 to 6 hours  |  **GLUTEN FREE, VEGAN**

*Take your pick of short or long grain rice for this dish. You'll cook the rice and the beets separately. This bowl is named after a favorite ski run at Whitewater Ski Resort in Nelson, British Columbia; the recipe is adapted from Whitewater Cooks by Shelley Adams. Warning: the sauce is absolutely addictive.*

### Into the cooker:

1 cup brown rice, rinsed
1-3/4 cups water

4 medium beets, greens and
    roots trimmed off

### For the glory sauce:

1/2 cup olive oil
1/4 cup nutritional yeast flakes
1/4 cup tamari
    (wheat-free soy sauce)
1/4 cup apple cider vinegar
2 tablespoons tahini
1 clove garlic, crushed

### For the bowls:

2 cups loosely packed baby spinach
2 large carrots, coarsely grated
8 ounces firm or savory baked tofu,
    cubed
1/2 cup slivered toasted almonds

1. Cook the brown rice and the beets separately as directed on pages 86 and 87. Cut the beets into matchsticks.

2. Whisk together the olive oil, nutritional yeast, tamari, vinegar, tahini, and garlic.

3. Assemble the bowls by putting 1/4 of the rice in each bowl and evenly distributing the beets, spinach, carrots, tofu, and almonds. Top with plenty of the glory sauce.

# GREEK LENTIL BOWL

MAKES 4 | COOK 2 to 3 hours | **GLUTEN FREE, VEGETARIAN OR VEGAN**

*Built around lentils and quinoa, this bowl is easy to prepare, nourishing, and delicious. English cucumbers don't need to be peeled or seeded; if you use a regular slicing cucumber, be sure to peel and seed it.*

**Into the cooker:**
1 cup dried green or brown lentils
2 cups water

1/2 cup quinoa, rinsed
3/4 cup water

**For the lemon tahini sauce:**
6 tablespoons tahini
1/4 cup water
1/4 cup olive oil
3 tablespoons fresh lemon juice
1 clove garlic, pressed
1 tablespoon fresh mint or
    1-1/2 teaspoons dried mint
1 teaspoon maple syrup
1/2 teaspoon salt

**For the bowls:**
2 cups loosely packed salad greens
1 medium English cucumber, halved
    lengthwise and thinly sliced
1-1/2 cups halved cherry tomatoes

1 cup crumbled feta cheese,
    dairy or nondairy
1/2 cup walnut pieces
1/2 cup sliced kalamata olives
thinly sliced red onion or fresh mint

1.  Cook the lentils and the quinoa separately as directed on pages 86 and 87.

2.  Whisk together the tahini, water, olive oil, lemon juice, garlic, mint, maple syrup, and salt.

3.  Assemble the bowls by putting 1/4 of the salad greens in each bowl and evenly distributing the lentils, quinoa, cucumber, cherry tomatoes, feta, walnut pieces, olives, and red onion or mint. Top with plenty of the lemon tahini sauce.

# CHIMICHURRI BOWL

SERVES 4  |  COOK 2 to 3 hours  |  **GLUTEN FREE, VEGAN**

*This combination of basmati rice, sweet potatoes, and black beans with dollops of spicy green chimichurri sauce is appealing to the eye and very toothsome and filling.*

**Into the cooker:**
2 medium orange-fleshed sweet potatoes, peeled and cut into 1/2-inch cubes

1 cup brown basmati rice, rinsed
1-3/4 cups water

**To finish the rice:**
1 tablespoon olive oil
juice of 1 lime
1/4 teaspoon salt

**For the chimichurri sauce:**
1 cup packed fresh cilantro
1 cup packed fresh parsley
2 cloves garlic, chopped
1/3 cup olive oil
2 tablespoons chopped fresh oregano
2 tablespoons fresh lime juice
2 tablespoons red wine vinegar
1 teaspoon salt
a pinch of red chili flakes

**For the bowls:**
2 (15-ounce) cans black beans, drained and rinsed

2 tablespoons minced red onion
2 teaspoons red wine vinegar
1/2 teaspoon smoked paprika
1/2 teaspoon salt
2 cups loosely packed salad greens
1 avocado, sliced

1.  Cook the sweet potatoes and the rice as directed on pages 86 and 87. Stir the olive oil, lime juice, and salt into the cooked and cooled rice.

2.  In a blender, puree the cilantro, parsley, garlic, olive oil, oregano, lime juice, vinegar, salt, and chili flakes until smooth.

3.  In a medium bowl, toss the black beans with the onion, vinegar, paprika, and salt. Assemble the bowls by putting 1/4 of the salad greens in each bowl and evenly distributing the sweet potatoes, rice, and beans. Top with avocado slices and plenty of the chimichurri sauce.

# MOROCCAN GRAIN BOWL

MAKES 4  |  COOK 2 to 3 hours  |  **GLUTEN FREE, VEGAN**

*This refreshing and nourishing bowl uses harissa, Tunisian hot chili pepper paste. For more protein, add crumbled (dairy or nondairy) feta cheese to the mix.*

### Into the cooker:
1 cup dried green or brown lentils
2 cups water
2 medium carrots, grated
1 fennel bulb, trimmed and
    diced small

1 cup quinoa, rinsed
1-1/2 cups water

### For the spicy harissa sauce:
1/2 cup olive oil
zest from 1 orange
    (about 1 teaspoon)
6 tablespoons orange juice
2 tablespoons apple cider vinegar
2 tablespoons harissa
1 teaspoon Dijon mustard
1/2 teaspoon ground coriander
1/2 teaspoon salt
2 cloves garlic, pressed

### For the bowls:
2 cups arugula
1/4 cup fresh mint, chopped
1/4 cup dried currants
toasted pumpkin seeds,
    sunflower seeds, and/or
    pine nuts for garnish

1. Cook the lentils (with the grated carrots and the fennel stirred in) and the quinoa separately as directed on pages 86 and 87. Allow to cool.

2. Whisk together the olive oil, orange zest, orange juice, vinegar, harissa, mustard, coriander, salt, and garlic.

3. Assemble the bowls by putting 1/4 of the arugula in each bowl and evenly distributing the lentils, quinoa, mint, currants, and seeds or nuts. Top with plenty of the spicy harissa sauce.

# GREEN GODDESS BOWL

MAKES 4  |  COOK 2 to 3 hours  |  **VEGAN**

*Garbanzos and chewy farro (an ancient grain that contains less gluten than modern wheat) are a really satisfying combination in this bowl inspired by a recipe in* Power Plates *by Gina Hamshaw. Add crumbled (dairy or nondairy) feta cheese for more protein.*

**Into the cooker:**

1 cup pearled or hulled farro

1-3/4 cups water

**To mix with the cooked farro:**

15-ounce can garbanzos,
    drained and rinsed

1 stalk celery, finely chopped

1 medium carrot, grated

1 tablespoon chopped fresh
    dill weed or 1 teaspoon dried
    dill weed

1 tablespoon olive oil

2 teaspoons fresh lemon juice

1/4 teaspoon salt

**For the tahini green goddess dressing:**

1/4 cup water

1/4 cup tahini

2 tablespoons fresh lemon juice

1 tablespoon apple cider vinegar

1 teaspoon maple syrup

1/4 cup packed coarsely chopped
    fresh parsley

1/4 cup packed coarsely chopped
    fresh basil leaves

1/2 teaspoon salt

1 clove garlic, chopped

**For the bowls:**

2 cups loosely packed salad greens

1-1/2 cups halved cherry tomatoes

1 large ripe avocado, sliced

1.  Cook the farro as directed on page 86. Cool and transfer to a medium bowl. Add the garbanzos, celery, carrot, dill weed, olive oil, lemon juice, and salt, and stir gently until well combined.

2.  In a blender, puree the water, tahini, lemon juice, vinegar, maple syrup, parsley, basil, salt, and garlic until smooth.

3.  Assemble the bowls by putting 1/4 of the salad greens in each bowl and evenly distributing the farro mixture, cherry tomatoes, and avocado slices. Top with plenty of the green goddess dressing.

# HIGHWAY TO KALE BOWL

MAKES 4  |  COOK 2 to 3 hours  |  **VEGETARIAN**

*This bowl is truly simple to make and very flavorful, and it uses the kale that's sometimes begging to be harvested in the garden. It was inspired by a recipe in* Adventures in Slow Cooking *by Sarah DiGregorio.*

**Into the cooker:**
1-1/2 cups pearled or hulled farro
2-1/2 cups water

**For the marinated kale:**
1 bunch lacinato or red leaf kale, stemmed and cut into thin ribbons (about 2 cups)
3 tablespoons olive oil
3 tablespoons fresh lemon juice
1 tablespoon snipped fresh chives
1/2 teaspoon salt
1/4 teaspoon red pepper flakes

**For the bowls:**
1/2 cup finely grated pecorino cheese
1/2 cup chopped smoked almonds

1. Place the farro and water in a dark baking pan and swish briefly to combine. Cover and place in the solar cooker. Bake until the grain is tender and the water has been absorbed, 2 to 3 hours. Remove from the cooker and fluff with a fork.

2. Place the kale, olive oil, lemon juice, chives, salt, and red pepper flakes in a sealable bag or container. Massage the ingredients together well and let sit for at least 1/2 hour, or up to a day if kept in the fridge.

3. Assemble the bowls by putting 1/4 of the farro in each bowl and evenly distributing the marinated kale, pecorino, and almonds.

# MANGO SHRIMP AND BLACK RICE BOWL

SERVES 4 | COOK 2 to 3 hours | **GLUTEN FREE**

*The shrimp and black rice cook separately and the shrimp can be put in the cooker later since it takes less time to bake. Black rice has a nice chewy texture and looks striking as a backdrop for the other colors in this bowl. The mango sauce is to die for. I use leftover sauce on a half avocado for lunch.*

### Into the cooker:

1 cup black rice, rinsed

1-3/4 cups water

1 pound uncooked jumbo shrimp, deveined and peeled or unpeeled, rinsed and patted dry

### For the mango sauce:

1 ripe mango, peeled and cut into chunks

1/2 cup avocado oil

1/2 cup fresh lime juice

2 teaspoons cumin

1 teaspoon salt

### For the bowls:

2 large ripe avocados, cut into small chunks

4 radishes, thinly sliced

1 red bell pepper, julienned, or sliced fresh pineapple

1/4 cup chopped cilantro

1. Cook the rice and the shrimp separately as directed on pages 86 and 87.

2. In a blender, puree the mango, oil, lime juice, cumin, and salt until smooth.

3. Assemble the bowls by putting 1/4 of the rice in each bowl and evenly distributing the shrimp, avocado, radishes, bell pepper or pineapple, and cilantro. Top with plenty of the mango sauce.

# SESAME SALMON AND BLACK RICE BOWL

MAKES 4  |  COOK 2 to 3 hours  |  **GLUTEN FREE**

*The salmon and black rice cook separately, and the salmon can be put in the cooker later since it takes less time to bake. The recipe makes plenty of miso sesame sauce, which you'll be glad to have. I've served this dish to company for Sunday dinner and gotten rave reviews every time.*

**Into the cooker:**

1 cup black rice, rinsed

1-3/4 cups water

1 pound salmon fillets

1 teaspoon toasted sesame oil

**To finish the rice:**

2 tablespoons minced red onion

1 teaspoon toasted sesame oil

**For the miso sesame sauce:**

1/2 cup water

1/2 cup miso

2 tablespoons avocado oil

2 tablespoons maple syrup

2 tablespoons apple cider vinegar

2 teaspoons toasted sesame oil

**For the bowls:**

8 large red radishes,
    halved and thinly sliced

2 large ripe avocados, sliced

1/4 cup chopped cilantro

1 teaspoon sesame seeds

1. Rinse the salmon and pat dry, then rub with the sesame oil. Cook the salmon and the black rice separately as directed on pages 86 and 87. Mix the onion and the sesame oil into the cooked and cooled rice.

2. Whisk together the water, miso, avocado oil, maple syrup, vinegar, and sesame oil until smooth.

3. Assemble the bowls by putting 1/4 of the rice in each bowl and evenly distributing the salmon, radishes, avocado, and cilantro. Sprinkle with the sesame seeds. Top generously with the miso sesame sauce.

# CHICKEN CURRY BOWL

MAKES 4  |  COOK 2 to 3 hours  |  **GLUTEN FREE**

*Another favorite around here. You can put together the fabulous curry sauce, inspired by a recipe in* Whole Bowls *by Allison Day, in the morning or just before dinner.*

### Into the cooker:
1 pound boneless and skinless
    chicken breasts

1 cup brown jasmine rice, rinsed
1-3/4 cups water

### For the curry sauce:
6 tablespoons tahini
1/4 cup fresh lemon juice
5 tablespoons water
2 tablespoons maple syrup
2 tablespoons nutritional yeast
1 tablespoon curry powder
1 teaspoon salt
a grind of black pepper

### For the bowls:
2 cups shredded green cabbage
2 medium carrots, coarsely grated
1/2 cup unsalted peanuts
1/4 cup minced candied ginger
1/4 cup coarsely chopped mint

1. Cook the chicken and the rice separately as directed on pages 86 and 87.

2. Whisk together the tahini, lemon juice, water, maple syrup, nutritional yeast, curry powder, salt, and black pepper.

3. Assemble the bowls by putting 1/4 of the rice in each bowl and evenly distributing the chicken, cabbage, carrots, peanuts, ginger, and mint. Top with plenty of the curry sauce.

# CHIPOTLE-HONEY CHICKEN BOWL

MAKES 4  |  COOK 2 to 3 hours  |  **GLUTEN FREE**

*Canned chipotles and honey combine to give the shredded chicken a sweet-spicy flavor. It doesn't hurt to leave the chicken in the cooker all day.*

**Into the cooker:**
1-1/4 to 1-1/2 pounds boneless,
    skinless chicken thighs,
    fat trimmed
1/4 cup honey
1/4 cup minced red onion
1 chipotle from a can of chipotle
    peppers in adobo sauce,
    finely chopped
1 tablespoon adobo sauce
1 teaspoon garlic powder
1 teaspoon salt

1 cup brown jasmine rice, rinsed
1-3/4 cups water

**For the mayo-lime sauce:**
1/3 cup mayonnaise
3 tablespoons fresh lime juice
1/2 teaspoon salt

**For the bowls:**
15-ounce can black beans, drained
    and rinsed
2 cups shredded green cabbage
1 large avocado, sliced

2 medium tomatoes, seeded and
    finely diced
fresh cilantro sprigs

1. Place the chicken, honey, onion, chipotle, adobo sauce, garlic powder, and salt in a dark baking pan, stir well, and cook as directed on page 87. Cook the brown rice as directed on page 86. Shred the cooked chicken with two forks and mix well with the juices in the pan.

2. Whisk together the mayonnaise, lime juice, and salt until smooth.

3. Assemble the bowls by putting 1/4 of the rice in each bowl and evenly distributing the chicken with juices, black beans, cabbage, avocado, tomato, and cilantro. Drizzle with the mayo-lime sauce.

# BARBACOA BURRITO BOWL

MAKES 4  |  COOK 6 to 8 hours  |  **GLUTEN FREE**

*Barbacoa is any meat that's cooked very slowly with flavor-enhancing herbs and spices for tender and succulent results. This recipe uses chuck roast, but you could also use beef stew meat or pork tenderloin. I always like to use meat that's pasture raised and locally sourced.*

### Into the cooker:
ingredients for Barbacoa Beef
　　(page 147)

1 cup brown jasmine or
　　basmati rice, rinsed
1-3/4 cups water or broth

### To finish the rice:
1 tablespoon olive oil
1/2 teaspoon salt
1 lime, juice and zest
1/4 cup finely chopped
　　fresh cilantro

### For the bowls:
15-ounce can pinto beans,
　　drained and rinsed
4 large red radishes, halved
　　and thinly sliced
2 large avocados, cubed
crumbled Cotija cheese,
　　pico de gallo, sour cream

1. Cook the Barbacoa Beef as directed on page 147 and the rice as directed on page 86.

2. Whisk together the oil, salt, lime juice, and lime zest, and pour over the rice. Add the cilantro and toss to mix well.

3. Assemble the bowls by putting 1/4 of the rice in each bowl and evenly distributing the barbacoa, pinto beans, radishes, and avocado. Crumble Cotija cheese over the top and garnish with pico de gallo and sour cream.

# Quiches and Casseroles

*Chicken Enchilada Casserole*

# GREEN CHILI QUICHE

SERVES 4 to 6  |  COOK 1 to 2 hours  |  **GLUTEN FREE, VEGETARIAN**

*Sometimes you want to go whole hog with the dairy, like when you're on a keto diet. This quick and easy recipe is for those times. Just be sure to balance it out with a big green salad on the side. Check the quiche at 1 hour and be sure not to overcook.*

4 6-inch corn tortillas, torn
    into about 6 pieces each
2 cups (8 ounces) grated
    cheddar cheese
2 cups (8 ounces) grated
    Monterey Jack cheese
8-ounce can (or two 4-ounce cans)
    diced green chilis, drained
6 eggs
1 cup sour cream or plain
    Greek yogurt

sliced avocado and/or tomato, pico
    de gallo, or salsa for garnish

1. Oil a dark 9-3/4-inch-round roaster and distribute the tortilla pieces evenly in the bottom to cover. Then sprinkle the grated cheeses and the chilis evenly over this layer.

2. In a large mixing bowl, whisk together the eggs and sour cream or yogurt. Pour the mixture over the cheeses and chilis in the pan. Cover and bake in the solar cooker until firmly set, 1 to 2 hours.

3. Allow to cool slightly before cutting into wedges to serve. Garnish with sliced avocado and/or tomato, pico de gallo, or salsa.

# CRUSTLESS CRAB QUICHE

SERVES 4  |  COOK 1 to 2 hours  |  **GLUTEN FREE**

*Although quiches are easy and quick to make in a solar cooker, the usual pastry crust doesn't fare well at low temperatures. Consequently, a couple of the quiches here have unusual crusts and a couple have none. This crustless quiche goes together quickly and tastes delicious. Check this at 1 hour and be sure not to overcook. Serve with a big green salad and some crusty bread.*

4 eggs

1 cup sour cream or plain
  Greek yogurt

1 cup small curd cottage cheese
  or ricotta

1 cup grated Parmesan cheese

1 cup (4 ounces) grated
  Monterey Jack cheese

3/4 cup shredded crab meat

1/4 cup thinly sliced green onions

1.  Oil a dark 9-3/4-inch-round roaster.

2.  In a large mixing bowl, beat together the eggs, sour cream or yogurt, and cottage cheese or ricotta. Stir in the cheeses, crab, and green onions. Scrape the mixture into the pan. Cover and bake in the solar cooker until firmly set, 1 to 2 hours.

3.  Allow to cool slightly before cutting into wedges to serve.

# PEAR AND GORGONZOLA QUICHE

**SERVES 4  |  COOK 1 to 2 hours  |  GLUTEN FREE, VEGETARIAN**

*The crust of this yummy quiche is made of walnut pieces. Check the quiche at 1 hour and be sure not to overcook. Pairs well with buttery croissants and a big green salad.*

1 cup walnut pieces

1 large or 2 medium ripe Bartlett or Bosc pears, cored and cut into slices

1-1/2 cups (6 ounces) crumbled Gorgonzola cheese

6 eggs

1 cup cream

1. Oil a dark 9-3/4-inch-round roaster and sprinkle the walnut pieces in an even layer in the bottom of the pan. Evenly distribute the sliced pear in a single layer over the walnut pieces. Scatter the Gorgonzola crumbles evenly over the pear slices.

2. In a large mixing bowl, whisk together the eggs and cream. Pour over the pear slices and cheese in the pan. Cover and bake in the solar cooker until firmly set, 1 to 2 hours.

3. Allow to cool slightly before cutting into wedges to serve.

# SMOKED SALMON AND GOAT CHEESE QUICHE

SERVES 4  |  COOK 1 to 2 hours  |  **GLUTEN FREE**

*This quiche has no crust, so serve it with crusty bread and a big green salad. Check the quiche at 1 hour and be sure not to overcook.*

6 eggs

1 cup sour cream or plain Greek yogurt

1 tablespoon chopped fresh dill weed or 1 teaspoon dried dill weed

1/2 teaspoon salt

4 ounces hot-smoked salmon filets (not lox), flaked

1/3 cup thinly sliced green onions

5 ounces goat cheese

1. Oil a dark 9-3/4-inch-round roaster.

2. In a large mixing bowl, beat together the eggs, sour cream or yogurt, dill, and salt. Stir in the flaked salmon and green onions. Pour the mixture into the pan. Crumble the goat cheese evenly over the mixture. Cover and bake in the solar cooker until firmly set, 1 to 2 hours.

3. Allow to cool slightly before cutting into wedges to serve.

# SPINACH AND SUN-DRIED TOMATO FRITTATA

SERVES 4 | COOK 1 to 2 hours | **GLUTEN FREE, VEGETARIAN**

*Quiches and frittatas are close cousins, and since frittatas officially have no crusts and are kind of like an omelet, they take well to solar cooking. The spinach in this recipe cooks down quite nicely from its raw state. Just pile it in and press it down. Check this dish at 1 hour and be sure not to overcook.*

4 cups firmly packed baby spinach (5 ounces)

1 cup (4 ounces) crumbled feta cheese, divided

1/2 cup grated Parmesan cheese, divided

1/4 cup minced oil-marinated sun-dried tomatoes

1/4 cup chopped fresh basil

8 eggs

1/2 cup half and half

1/2 teaspoon salt

1/8 teaspoon ground black pepper

1. Oil a dark 9-3/4-inch-round roaster and spread half the spinach in the bottom of the pan in an even layer to cover. Then evenly sprinkle in 1/2 cup feta, 1/4 cup Parmesan, all the sun-dried tomatoes, and the basil. Add one more layer of spinach, then the remaining cheese.

2. In a large mixing bowl, whisk together the eggs, half and half, salt, and pepper. Pour the mixture into the pan. Cover and bake in the solar cooker until firmly set, 1 to 2 hours.

3. Allow to cool slightly before cutting into wedges to serve.

# ZUCCHINI AND RED PEPPER FRITTATA

SERVES 4  |  COOK 4 to 6 hours  |  **VEGETARIAN**

*This frittata comes out beautifully if you cook the veggies in advance of adding the eggs and cheese. The key is to get the veggies to release their liquid and then to drain it off so the frittata doesn't get watery. This pairs well with Quinoa Tabouli for an easy hot day meal.*

### Into the cooker first:

4 cups finely diced zucchini (about 3 medium zucchini)

1/2 cup minced red bell pepper

1/4 cup finely minced purple onion

### Add to the cooker later:

3 large eggs

1 cup mayonnaise

1 teaspoon smoked paprika

1-1/4 cups grated Parmesan cheese, divided

1. Place the zucchini, pepper, and onion in a dark 9-3/4-inch-round roaster. Cover and bake in the solar cooker until the veggies start to get tender, 2 to 3 hours. Then drain the pan and dump the veggies onto a clean dish towel to drain further. Oil the pan well and place the drained veggies back in it.

2. In a large mixing bowl, whisk the eggs, mayonnaise, and paprika until smooth, then stir in 1 cup Parmesan cheese. Scrape into the pan and level the surface. Sprinkle the remaining 1/4 cup Parmesan evenly over the surface. Bake covered in the solar cooker until firmly set in the middle, 2 to 3 hours or longer.

3. Allow to cool slightly before cutting into wedges to serve.

# SPANISH TORTILLA WITH RED PEPPER AIOLI

**SERVES 4  |  COOK 5 to 6 hours  |  GLUTEN FREE, VEGETARIAN**

*A traditional Spanish tortilla is basically an onion and potato frittata. This one has Manchego cheese added for extra protein and flavor. It's best served at room temperature. In the solar cooker, there are two stages: cooking the potatoes and onions, and then adding the eggs and cheese and cooking again. Serve it with a green salad or slaw to make a full meal. Recipe adapted from* Adventures in Slow Cooking *by Sarah DiGregorio.*

### Into the cooker first:

4 medium Yukon Gold potatoes, sliced 1/4 inch thick

1 yellow onion, halved and thinly sliced

2 tablespoons olive oil

1/2 teaspoon salt

### Add to the cooker later:

1 cup (4 ounces) grated Manchego cheese

6 eggs

1 tablespoon milk or plain unsweetened nondairy milk

1/2 teaspoon salt

a grind of black pepper

### For the red pepper aioli:

3 tablespoons minced roasted red peppers from a jar

1 small clove garlic, finely grated or pressed

1/2 cup mayonnaise

1. Place the potatoes and onion in a dark 9-3/4-inch-round roaster and toss with the oil and 1/2 teaspoon salt. Cover and bake in the solar cooker until the onion is tender when tested with a fork, 3 to 4 hours. Remove from the cooker. Drain any cooking liquid and oil the sides of the pan.

2. Evenly distribute the cheese over the potatoes and onion. In a mixing bowl, beat the eggs, milk, 1/2 teaspoon salt, and pepper, then pour evenly over the potatoes, onion, and cheese in the pan. Cover and bake in the solar cooker until firmly set, 2 hours or so. Do not overcook. Allow to cool slightly before cutting into wedges to serve.

3. To make the aioli, stir the peppers, garlic, and mayonnaise together in a small bowl. Top the tortilla wedges with a generous dollop.

# CHICKEN ENCHILADA CASSEROLE

SERVES 4 to 6  |  COOK 3 to 5 hours  |  **GLUTEN FREE**

*Enchilada casseroles are much easier to put together than individual enchiladas and they taste just the same, so they're a go-to solar meal around here. Make this casserole in two stages: first cook the chicken breasts, then the casserole.*

1 pound boneless and skinless chicken breasts

1 cup plain yogurt

1/4 cup water

1/4 cup tomato paste

7-ounce can diced green chilis, drained

4-ounce can sliced black olives, drained

1 teaspoon dried oregano

1/2 teaspoon ground cumin

1/2 teaspoon chili powder

1/4 teaspoon salt

8 6-inch corn tortillas

2 cups (8 ounces) shredded cheddar and/or Monterey Jack cheese, divided

pico de gallo, sliced avocado, and sour cream for garnish

1.  Place the chicken breasts in a dark baking pan. Cover and bake in the solar cooker until no longer pink, 1 to 2 hours. Remove, cool, and shred.

2.  In a large bowl, whisk together the yogurt, water, and tomato paste. Then stir in the chilis, olives, oregano, cumin, chili powder, and salt.

3.  Cover the bottom of a dark 9-inch-square pan with 1/3 of the yogurt mixture. Tear 4 of the tortillas into large pieces and scatter evenly over this mixture, then cover evenly with the shredded chicken, 1-1/2 cups of the cheese, and another 1/3 of the mixture. Top with the remaining tortillas torn into large pieces, yogurt mixture, and cheese.

4.  Cover and bake in the solar cooker until the cheese has melted, 2 to 3 hours. Allow to cool slightly before cutting and adding garnishes.

# SWEET POTATO AND BLACK BEAN ENCHILADA CASSEROLE

SERVES 4 to 6  |  COOK 3 to 5 hours  |  **GLUTEN FREE, VEGETARIAN**

*This hearty and filling casserole goes together quickly. Do this in two stages: first cook the sweet potato, then the casserole.*

2 medium orange-fleshed sweet potatoes, peeled and cut into 1/4-inch rounds

15-ounce can red enchilada sauce

8 6-inch corn tortillas

15-ounce can black beans, drained and rinsed

4-ounce can diced green chilis, drained

4-ounce can sliced black olives, drained

2 cups (8 ounces) shredded Mexican blend cheese

chopped fresh cilantro, sliced avocado, pico de gallo, and sour cream for garnish

1.  Put the sweet potato rounds in a dark baking pan. Cover and bake in the solar cooker until just barely tender when tested with a fork, 1 to 2 hours.

2.  In the bottom of a dark 9-inch-square pan, spread 1/2 cup of the enchilada sauce. Tear 3 of the tortillas into large pieces and scatter evenly. Evenly distribute half of the sweet potato rounds, beans, chilis, and olives, followed by half of the cheese and 1/2 cup of the enchilada sauce. Scatter 3 more torn tortillas and the rest of the beans, chilis, and olives. Finish with 2 more torn tortillas and the remaining enchilada sauce, sweet potato rounds, and cheese.

3.  Cover and bake in the solar cooker until the cheese has melted, 2 to 3 hours. Allow to cool slightly before cutting.

4.  Garnish each serving with cilantro, avocado, pico de gallo, and sour cream.

# ZITI BAKED WITH THREE CHEESES AND FRESH HERBS

SERVES 4  |  COOK 3 to 4 hours  |  **VEGETARIAN**

*This is pure keto comfort food. You mix the dry uncooked pasta with a soupy sauce before setting it in the sun to meld with the fresh flavors of herbs and three different cheeses. You can use traditional wheat pasta or any gluten-free variety. Use prepared marinara sauce or make your own the day before (see the recipe for Garden Fresh Marinara in Basics and Bonus Recipes). Have fun with the herbs and throw in more if they're growing rampant in your garden. Serve with a big green and/or fruit salad.*

1-3/4 cups marinara sauce

8 ounces sour cream

3/4 cup water

1/2 cup chopped fresh parsley

1/2 cup chopped fresh oregano

1/4 cup sliced Kalamata olives

1 cup (4 ounces) shredded
    mozzarella cheese

1 cup grated Parmesan cheese,
    divided

8 ounces dry uncooked ziti
    or other tubular pasta

1 large ripe tomato, sliced

1 cup (4 ounces) shredded Havarti
    or fontina cheese

1/4 cup chopped fresh basil
    for topping

1. In a large mixing bowl, whisk together the marinara, sour cream, and water. Stir in the parsley, oregano, olives, mozzarella, and 1/2 cup of the Parmesan cheese. Add the ziti and combine evenly.

2. Oil a dark 9-inch-square pan. Scrape the pasta mixture into the pan and distribute evenly, smoothing the surface and making sure all the pasta is tucked into the sauce. Distribute sliced tomato evenly over surface. Sprinkle with the Havarti or fontina and the remaining 1/2 cup Parmesan cheese.

3. Cover and bake 3 to 4 hours in the solar cooker. Allow the pasta to rest for 20 minutes before cutting into squares and serving with fresh basil sprinkled on top.

# BUTTERNUT SQUASH, SUN-DRIED TOMATO, AND SPINACH LASAGNA

SERVES 4 to 6  |  COOK 4 to 6 hours or all day  |  **VEGETARIAN**

*Yes, you can cook pasta in the solar cooker, but not in the usual way. The noodles go in raw and soak up the liquid from the other ingredients as the dish cooks slowly and gently. You don't even need to use no-cook noodles. Using prepared Alfredo sauce is a time saver. The longer you can leave this dish in the cooker, the better.*

1 egg

1-1/4 cups grated Parmesan cheese, divided

1 cup ricotta cheese

1/4 cup minced oil-marinated sun-dried tomatoes

1 tablespoon Italian seasoning

1/2 teaspoon salt

15-ounce jar Alfredo sauce

1 medium butternut squash (about 2 pounds), peeled, seeded, quartered lengthwise, and sliced very thin

3 cups (about 4 ounces) firmly packed baby spinach

6 dry uncooked lasagna noodles, wheat or other

1. In a large mixing bowl, beat the egg, then mix in 1 cup of the Parmesan cheese, the ricotta, and the sun-dried tomatoes, Italian seasoning, and salt.

2. In the bottom of a dark 9-inch-square pan, spread 1/2 cup of the Alfredo sauce. Then arrange 1/3 of the squash slices in a thin layer and distribute 1/3 of the spinach evenly. Ever-so-carefully dollop and spread 1/3 of the cheese mixture on top of this layer, using your fingers if necessary. Break 2 noodles into pieces and evenly cover the cheese with them.

3. Add a second layer of 1/4 cup Alfredo sauce, using your spoon to swoosh it over the noodles, and then 1/3 of the squash, spinach, and cheese mixture. Break 2 more noodles into pieces and evenly cover the cheese with them.

4. Add a third layer of 1/4 cup Alfredo sauce plus the remaining squash, spinach, and cheese mixture. Break 2 more noodles into pieces and evenly cover the cheese with them. Press everything down firmly and then spread the rest of the Alfredo sauce (about 3/4 cup) over all, making sure all the noodles are covered with sauce. Sprinkle evenly with the remaining 1/4 cup Parmesan cheese.

5. Cover and bake 4 to 6 hours or longer in the solar cooker. Allow the lasagna to rest for 20 minutes before cutting into squares.

# ZUCCHINI, CARROT, AND SPINACH LASAGNA

SERVES 4 to 6  |  COOK 4 to 6 hours or all day  | **VEGETARIAN**

*In late summer, I make this every week to keep up with the zucchini coming in. It takes me about half an hour to put together, time well spent because it turns out so juicy and flavorful. Using prepared marinara sauce saves time, but you could also make your own the day before (see the recipe for Garden Fresh Marinara in Basics and Bonus Recipes). The longer this dish stays in the cooker, the better.*

1 egg

1-1/4 cups grated Parmesan cheese, divided

1 cup ricotta cheese

1 tablespoon Italian seasoning

1/2 teaspoon salt

1-3/4 cups marinara sauce

2 medium zucchini, sliced very thin

3 medium carrots, coarsely grated (about 3 cups)

3 cups (about 4 ounces) firmly packed baby spinach

6 dry uncooked lasagna noodles, wheat or other

1. In a large mixing bowl, beat the egg, then mix in 1 cup of the Parmesan cheese, the ricotta, and the Italian seasoning and salt.

2. In the bottom of a dark 9-inch-square pan, spread 1/2 cup of the marinara sauce. Then arrange 1/3 of the squash slices in a thin layer and distribute 1/3 of the carrots and then spinach evenly. Ever-so-carefully dollop and spread 1/3 of the cheese mixture on top of this layer, using your fingers if necessary. Break 2 noodles into pieces and evenly cover the cheese with them.

3. Add a second layer of 1/4 cup marinara, using your spoon to swoosh it over the noodles, and then 1/3 of the zucchini, carrot, spinach, and cheese mixture. Break 2 more noodles into pieces and evenly cover the cheese with them.

4. Add a third layer of 1/4 cup marinara plus the remaining zucchini, carrot, spinach, and cheese mixture. Break 2 more noodles into pieces and evenly cover the cheese with them. Press everything down firmly and then spread the rest of the marinara (3/4 cup) over all, making sure all the noodles are covered with sauce. Sprinkle evenly with the remaining 1/4 cup Parmesan cheese.

5. Cover and bake 4 to 6 hours or longer in the solar cooker. Allow the lasagna to rest for 20 minutes before cutting into squares.

# Sun-Baked Sweets

*Black Bean Brownies*

# BLACK BEAN BROWNIES

MAKES 16 brownies | COOK 3 to 4 hours | **GLUTEN FREE, VEGETARIAN**

*These good-for-you treats have lots of fiber and protein, and they're quick to make—no mixing bowl required! Because the batter is dark, you don't need to use a dark pan for this, but you can.*

15-ounce can black beans,
    drained and rinsed
1/2 cup maple syrup
1/3 cup quick rolled oats
1/3 cup avocado oil
1/3 cup creamy almond butter
2 eggs
2 tablespoons unsweetened
    cocoa powder
2 teaspoons vanilla extract
1/8 teaspoon salt
3/4 cup dark chocolate chips
    (I like stevia-sweetened ones)
1/2 cup diced almonds
    or walnut pieces

1. In a large blender container, puree the black beans, maple syrup, oats, oil, almond butter, eggs, cocoa powder, vanilla extract, and salt until smooth. Stir in the chocolate chips and almonds or walnuts.

2. Oil a 7-by-11-inch baking pan. Scrape the batter into the pan and spread out evenly by patting with the back of a large spoon.

3. Bake uncovered in the solar cooker until a toothpick inserted into the center comes out clean, 3 to 4 hours. Allow to cool before cutting into bars.

*To cook foods such as brownies and nuts uncovered inside an oven bag in a panel cooker, it's helpful to lay a dark grill mat over the pan to hold in the heat and prevent the oven bag from collapsing on the food. This isn't a problem with the Haines panel cooker as the flexible plastic insulating shell stands well off the food.*

# CARROT (OR ZUCCHINI) AND BEET BROWNIES

MAKES 16 brownies  |  COOK 3 to 4 hours  |  **GLUTEN FREE, VEGETARIAN**

*Raw grated veggies make these brownies moist and full of fiber while contributing to their rich flavor. If you have zucchini coming out of your ears, you can substitute zucchini for the carrot. The batter is dark, so you don't need a dark pan, but it doesn't hurt to use one.*

2 cups almond flour

1/4 cup unsweetened cocoa powder

1 teaspoon ground cinnamon

1 teaspoon baking soda

1/4 teaspoon salt

2 eggs

1/2 cup maple syrup

1/4 cup avocado oil

1 medium beet, peeled and coarsely grated

1 medium carrot (or zucchini), coarsely grated

1/2 cup dark chocolate chips (I like stevia-sweetened ones)

1/2 cup walnut or pecan pieces, or diced almonds

1. In a large mixing bowl, thoroughly combine the flour, cocoa powder, cinnamon, baking soda, and salt.

2. In a small bowl, whisk together the eggs, maple syrup, and oil. Add to the dry ingredients and stir to moisten well. Stir in the beet, carrot or zucchini, chocolate chips, and nuts.

3. Oil a 7-by-11-inch baking pan. Scrape the batter into the pan and spread out evenly by patting with the back of a large spoon.

4. Bake uncovered in the solar cooker until a toothpick inserted into the center comes out clean, 3 to 4 hours. Allow to cool before cutting into bars.

# LEMON SHORTCAKE BARS

**MAKES 16 bars | COOK 3 to 4 hours | GLUTEN FREE, VEGETARIAN OR VEGAN**

*These bars are moist, dense, and packed with flavor and protein. They're lemony and not overly sweet. Eat them like shortcake, topped with plain yogurt or whipped cream and berries, or take them along as trail or picnic food. See the recipe for Applesauce as Nature Intended in Basics and Bonus Recipes if you prefer to make your own rather than use store-bought applesauce.*

4 cups almond flour

3/4 cup xylitol or granulated
    monk fruit sweetener

1/2 teaspoon salt

1/2 cup plain yogurt,
    dairy or nondairy

1/2 cup applesauce

1/2 cup fresh lemon juice

1 tablespoon lemon zest

1.  In a large mixing bowl, thoroughly combine the flour, sweetener, and salt.

2.  In a separate bowl, whisk together the yogurt, applesauce, lemon juice, and lemon zest. Add to the dry ingredients and stir to combine evenly.

3.  Oil a dark 7-by-11-inch baking pan. Scrape the batter into the pan and spread out evenly by patting with the back of a large spoon.

4.  Bake uncovered in the solar cooker until a toothpick inserted into the center comes out clean, 3 to 4 hours. Allow to cool before cutting into bars.

# BANANA PEANUT BUTTER BARS

MAKES 16 bars | COOK 2 to 3 hours | **GLUTEN FREE, VEGAN**

*These chewy and moist bars are easy to tuck into a backpack or picnic basket. To mash the bananas, I cut them up into little pieces and then smash them with a potato masher. If you can't find almond meal, you can substitute almond flour. These bars can be stored at room temperature for a few days, and they actually taste better and better as they age.*

2 cups quick rolled oats
1/2 cup almond meal
1/2 cup finely shredded
    unsweetened coconut
1/8 teaspoon salt
3 large ripe bananas, well mashed
    (1 to 1-1/2 cups)
1 cup crunchy peanut butter
1/2 cup maple syrup

1. In a large mixing bowl, thoroughly combine the oats, almond meal, coconut, and salt.

2. In a separate bowl, mix together the bananas, peanut butter, and maple syrup. Add to the dry ingredients and stir to combine evenly.

3. Oil a dark 7-by-11-inch baking pan. Scrape the batter into the pan and spread out evenly by patting with the back of a large spoon.

4. Bake uncovered in the solar cooker until a toothpick inserted into the center comes out clean, 2 to 3 hours. Allow to cool before cutting into bars.

# FROZEN BARK

MAKES about 16 pieces  |  COOK 1 hour or less  |  **GLUTEN FREE, VEGAN**

*I know you didn't expect to find something with "frozen" in the title in a solar oven cookbook, but it turns out the solar cooker is ideal for melting things like coconut oil and chocolate chips. Stir them up with a couple of other ingredients and the resulting delicious little energy snacks are completely addictive. Once you take them out of the freezer to eat, they melt pretty fast, so eat 'em right away.*

**For almond butter bark:**
1/4 cup coconut oil
1 cup creamy almond butter
2 tablespoons maple syrup
1/2 teaspoon ground cinnamon
1/4 teaspoon vanilla extract

**For chocolate-cherry-pecan bark:**
1/4 cup coconut oil
1 cup dark chocolate chips
    (I like stevia-sweetened ones)
1/2 cup dried cherries,
    finely chopped
1/2 cup pecan pieces

1. Place the coconut oil and the almond butter or chocolate chips in a dark baking pan. Cover and heat in the solar cooker until the oil and chocolate have melted, 1 hour or less.

2. Add the remaining ingredients for the bark of your choice and stir until smooth. Then put the whole pan into the freezer for several hours.

3. Turn the frozen mixture out of the pan by taking a dinner knife and cutting gently across the middle, then prying each side up. Break or cut into small pieces. Store these pieces in a plastic bag or airtight container in the freezer.

# SPICY CHOCOLATE NUTS

MAKES 4 cups | COOK 2 to 3 hours | **GLUTEN FREE, VEGAN**

*These irresistible chocolate-coated nuts are actually good for you. I adapted the recipe from Jennifer Iserloh's* The Healing Slow Cooker. *The baking works really well if done in a Haines cooker, since the flexible plastic cover stands off the pan so air can circulate and steam can escape. You can also bake the nuts in a box cooker with the lid propped open slightly to allow steam to escape.*

1/3 cup unsweetened cocoa powder

1/4 cup maple syrup

2 tablespoons avocado oil

2 teaspoons vanilla extract

1/2 teaspoon salt

1/2 teaspoon ground cloves

1/8 teaspoon ground cayenne pepper

4 cups any combination of raw unsalted walnut halves, pecan halves, and cashews

1. In a large mixing bowl, stir together the cocoa powder, maple syrup, oil, vanilla, salt, cloves, and cayenne until all the cocoa lumps are smoothed out. Add the nuts and toss until all are well coated.

2. Oil a dark rimmed baking sheet, ideally one big enough to accommodate all the nuts in a single layer. Transfer the nuts to the baking sheet and distribute them evenly.

3. Put the baking sheet into your solar cooker and leave until the coating on the nuts looks fairly dry, 2 to 3 hours. Allow to cool before storing in an airtight container at room temperature for up to a week.

# MEXICAN CHOCOLATE PUDDING

SERVES 4 to 6  |  COOK 1 to 2 hours  |  **GLUTEN FREE, VEGAN**

*This pudding, based on Mark Bittman's recipe in the* New York Times, *requires melting chocolate in sweetened water and is much simpler to prepare in a solar cooker than on the stovetop. I replace the cane sugar in the original recipe with powdered stevia. Because of the flavors involved, the stevia doesn't have the artificial taste it has in some dishes. My favorite part of making this pudding is licking the pan.*

1/4 cup powdered stevia
    (or 1/2 cup other sugar)
3/4 cup water
9-ounce bag dark chocolate chips
    (I like stevia-sweetened ones),
    divided
12 ounces soft silken tofu
1-1/2 teaspoons ground cinnamon
1 teaspoon vanilla extract
1/2 teaspoon chili powder

sliced fresh strawberries
    and/or mint leaves for garnish

1. Place the stevia or sugar and the water in a dark baking pan and stir until the sweetener is dissolved. Add all but a few of the chocolate chips (to be used later) and stir. Cover and cook in the solar cooker until the chocolate is melted, 1 to 2 hours. Stir until the mixture is smooth.

2. Pour the warm chocolate syrup into a large blender container and add the tofu, cinnamon, vanilla extract, and chili powder. Blend until smooth.

3. Scrape into 4 to 6 custard cups and refrigerate for at least 30 minutes before serving. Garnish with the reserved chocolate chips along with sliced strawberries and/or mint leaves.

# SWEET POTATO FUDGE PUDDING

SERVES 4  |  COOK 2 to 3 hours  |  **GLUTEN FREE, VEGAN**

*Cooked sweet potato gives this pudding a creamy texture, and almond butter makes it taste rich enough to call it fudge. It's a healthy no-guilt dessert. Note that the recipe calls for raw almond butter. This type of almond butter is runnier than butters made with roasted almonds. If you have only roasted almond butter on hand, just add a little water.*

2 medium orange-fleshed
    sweet potatoes
    (sometimes called yams)
1/4 cup maple syrup
1/4 cup plain unsweetened
    nondairy milk
1/4 cup unsweetened cocoa powder
1/4 cup raw creamy almond butter
1 teaspoon vanilla extract
1/4 teaspoon salt

sliced fresh strawberries
    and/or toasted pecan pieces
    for garnish

1.  Place the whole unpeeled sweet potatoes in a dark baking pan. Cover and bake in the solar cooker until tender when tested with a fork, 2 to 3 hours. Cool and scoop the flesh out of the skins into a small bowl. Mash and reserve 1-1/2 cups pulp.

2.  Place the sweet potato pulp in a large blender container with the maple syrup, nondairy milk, cocoa powder, almond butter, vanilla extract, and salt. Blend until smooth.

3.  Scrape into 4 custard cups and refrigerate for at least 30 minutes before serving. Garnish with sliced strawberries and/or pecan pieces.

# APPLE-GINGER OAT PUDDING

SERVES 4 to 6  |  COOK 4 to 5 hours  |  **GLUTEN FREE, VEGAN**

*The flavors of apple and ginger seem to me like a natural pairing. I like to bake this simple summertime comfort food for a really long time so the apples get very soft.*

1/2 cup steel cut oats

14-ounce can coconut milk (1-1/2 cups)

2 large apples, peeled, cored, and finely diced

3 tablespoons maple syrup

1 tablespoon finely grated fresh ginger

1 teaspoon vanilla extract

1. Stir the oats and coconut milk together in a dark baking pan, then stir in the apples, maple syrup, ginger, and vanilla. Cover and cook in the solar cooker until the apples have softened, 4 to 5 hours.

2. Serve warm or cooled.

# LIME-GINGER RICE PUDDING

SERVES 4 to 6  |  COOK 3 to 4 hours  |  **GLUTEN FREE, VEGAN**

*Rice pudding takes longer than just plain rice in the solar cooker because there's more liquid to bring up to cooking temperature. This version tastes great garnished with ripe nectarines, my favorite summertime fruit. You can also make a variation I call Golden Rice Pudding by replacing the lime juice and salt with 1 tablespoon turmeric, 2 teaspoons ground cinnamon, 1 pinch salt, and 1 pinch ground black pepper (which helps your body assimilate the good-for-you turmeric) and garnishing with banana slices and almond slivers.*

1 cup brown jasmine rice, rinsed

14-ounce can coconut milk (1-1/2 cups)

2-1/2 cups water

1/4 cup maple syrup

1/4 cup minced candied ginger

1/4 cup fresh lime juice

1/8 teaspoon salt

sliced nectarine, banana, or mango for garnish

1. Stir the rice, coconut milk, water, maple syrup, ginger, lime juice, and salt together in a dark baking pan. Press out the lumps as best you can with the back of a spoon. Cover and cook in the solar cooker until the rice is tender and the liquid has mostly been absorbed, 3 to 4 hours.

2. Stir and serve warm or cooled, garnished with nectarine, banana, or mango slices.

# STRAWBERRY-RHUBARB PUDDING

SERVES 4 to 6  |  COOK 1 to 2 hours  |  **GLUTEN FREE, VEGAN**

*With its huge leaves, rhubarb is a decorative addition to the garden. It does demand a lot of water to grow, but homegrown rhubarb is still less expensive than store-bought. The stalks need to be cooked with a sweetener to be edible.*

2 cups diced rhubarb stalks
2 cups halved strawberries
1/4 cup maple syrup
1 teaspoon vanilla extract
14-ounce can coconut cream,
    well mixed before adding
1/3 cup chia seeds

sliced strawberries and
    mint leaves for garnish

1. Place the rhubarb and strawberry pieces in a dark baking pan. Cover and cook in the solar cooker until the fruit is soft, 1 to 2 hours.

2. Let the fruit cool and transfer it to a small casserole, leaving the liquid (which will taste bitter) behind. Mash the fruit with a fork and then stir in the maple syrup, vanilla, coconut cream, and chia seeds.

3. Refrigerate 2 to 3 hours until firm. Serve garnished with sliced strawberries and mint leaves.

# SUMMER FRUIT CRUMBLE

SERVES 4 to 6  |  COOK 2 to 3 hours  |  **GLUTEN FREE, VEGAN**

*For this juicy crumble, you can use blueberries, cherries, raspberries, strawberries, boysenberries, apples, peaches, plums, apricots, or nectarines—whatever's in season. I tried using blueberries I had picked and then frozen, and the crumble turned out way too watery, so use only ripe fruit that hasn't been frozen. If you can't find almond meal, you can substitute almond flour.*

**For the crumble topping:**

1 cup almond meal

3/4 cup pecan pieces

1/4 cup coconut oil

1/4 cup maple syrup

1/4 cup fine shredded coconut

2 tablespoons flaxseed meal


6 cups (1-1/2 quarts) fresh
    or frozen fruit

2 tablespoons arrowroot powder
    or cornstarch

1 tablespoon honey

1 tablespoon fresh lemon
    or lime juice

1. In a medium bowl, mash together the almond meal, pecan pieces, oil, maple syrup, coconut, and flaxseed meal until uniformly moistened.

2. In a dark baking pan, gently stir together the fruit, arrowroot powder or cornstarch, honey, and lemon or lime juice. Crumble the topping mixture evenly over the fruit.

3. Bake uncovered in the solar cooker until bubbly and browned, 2 to 3 hours.

# BAKED APPLES WITH CASHEW CREAM

SERVES 4  |  COOK 2 to 4 hours  |  **GLUTEN FREE, VEGAN**

*This is an impressive healthy dessert or weekend brunch dish for company, and you can bake the apples a day ahead. Check at 2 hours to see how soft the apples are and give additional time depending on your texture preference. I've baked the apples almost to applesauce by leaving them in for 4 hours, and it only seemed to deepen the flavor. The dates and cinnamon combine with juices from the apples to produce a lovely sweet syrup to spoon over everything at the end of cooking. The cashew cream recipe makes about 1-1/2 cups, so you'll have some left over. You can store it in the fridge for up to 5 days and enjoy it on fruit or stirred into oatmeal.*

4 large baking apples,
    like Honeycrisp or Fuji
4 large or 6 small dates, pitted,
    chopped, soaked in hot water
    for at least 10 minutes
    and then drained
1-1/2 tablespoons coconut oil
1-1/2 teaspoons ground cinnamon
pinch of salt

**For the cashew cream:**
1 cup raw unsalted cashew
    pieces, soaked in water
    overnight or for at least
    1 hour and then drained
1/2 cup plain unsweetened
    nondairy milk
2 tablespoons maple syrup
1 teaspoon vanilla extract

1. Core the apples, being careful not to cut all the way through the bottoms. Place in a dark baking pan.

2. Using the back of a spoon, mash the dates, coconut oil, cinnamon, and salt to mix well. Spoon into the centers of the apples. Cover and bake in the solar cooker until the apples are tender, 2 to 4 hours.

3. In a blender, puree the cashews, nondairy milk, maple syrup, and vanilla until smooth. Spoon over the baked apples to serve.

# HONEY-RASPBERRY POACHED PEARS

SERVES 4 | COOK 1 to 2 hours | **GLUTEN FREE, VEGETARIAN OR VEGAN**

*These pears make a simple, tasty, and beautiful finish to any summer meal. Any kind of pear will work, and the cooking time depends on the ripeness. The hibiscus tea adds gorgeous color and flavor, and it will lower your blood pressure too.*

1/4 cup water

1 hibiscus tea bag, tag removed

2 large ripe or nearly ripe pears, such as D'Anjou or Bartlett

4 teaspoons honey, divided

1 cup fresh or frozen raspberries, divided

plain Greek yogurt, dairy or nondairy

1. Pour the water into a dark baking pan and place the tea bag in the middle, swishing it a little to saturate it.

2. Cut the pears in half lengthwise and scoop out the cores with a melon baller or spoon. (You can leave the stems.) Place cut side up in the pan.

3. Put 1 teaspoon of honey and 1/4 cup of raspberries in the hollow in each pear half. Cover and bake in the solar cooker until the pears are tender, 1 to 2 hours. Squeeze the tea bag into the pan and then discard.

4. To serve, chilled or warm, dollop some yogurt on each plate and spoon a pear half and some juice over it.

# SUMMER FRUIT COMPOTE

SERVES 6  |  COOK 3 to 4 hours  |  **GLUTEN FREE, VEGAN**

*Peaches, apricots, and plums all stew up really nicely with warming spices. You can peel them or just rinse them and leave them unpeeled before pitting and slicing 1/2 inch thick.*

5 cups sliced peaches, apricots, and/or plums

3 tablespoons honey or maple syrup

2 tablespoons red wine or water

1/8 teaspoon ground cinnamon

1/8 teaspoon ground cloves

1/8 teaspoon ground cardamom

1 thin slice lemon or lime

1. Place the fruit in a dark baking pan.

2. In a small bowl, combine the honey or maple syrup, the wine or water, and the cinnamon, cloves, and cardamom. Mix thoroughly and pour over the fruit. Add the lemon or lime slice.

3. Cover and bake in the solar cooker until the fruit is tender when tested with a fork, 3 to 4 hours.

# RHUBARB-APPLE OR PLUM-APPLE TOPPING SAUCE

MAKES 3 to 4 cups | COOK 1 to 2 hours | **GLUTEN FREE, VEGAN**

*These topping sauces make use of fruits you may have a lot of as they come into season. Serve over plain yogurt, frozen yogurt, or ice cream.*

### For rhubarb-apple topping sauce:

4 cups diced rhubarb stalks

2 cups tart apples that have been peeled, cored, and diced

1/4 cup maple syrup

1 teaspoon vanilla extract

### For plum-apple topping sauce:

3 cups apples that have been peeled, cored, and diced

3 cups ripe plums that have been pitted and halved

2 tablespoons maple syrup

2 tablespoons fresh lime juice

1. Place the fruit in a dark baking pan. Cover and cook in the solar cooker until the fruit is soft, about 1 hour. For the rhubarb-apple topping sauce, drain the liquid from the pan, as it's pretty bitter.

2. Mash the fruit with a fork or potato masher, and then stir in the additional ingredients.

# Basics and Bonus Recipes

**MY STRATEGY** for simple and tasty sun-baked meals is to cook up batches of staples that can serve as the basis of soups, salads, and bowls. These include carrots, beets, potatoes, sweet potatoes, grains, beans, and chicken breasts. You don't have to cook ahead like me, but a little basic knowledge about how to cook building block ingredients will help you think creatively about how to use your solar cooker to best fit your own style of cooking and eating.

## ROOT VEGETABLES

Root vegetables love slow cooking because it helps develop their flavors, and they are generally okay to put in the cooker and forget about. Give whole unpeeled vegetables at least 4 hours and up to all day. You can cook root vegetables in their skins in a dark baking pan with or without adding water; I find that about 1/4 inch of water in the bottom helps to steam them. You can also peel and cut up your root vegetables for faster cooking. If you do that, you can toss them with oil and/or herbs, or add a little water to steam.

To make veggie broth that you can later use to cook grains with, you can save your root vegetable scraps—garlic and onion peels, carrot and beet tops and peels, potato peels—along with broccoli stems, kale stalks, outer cabbage leaves, even apple cores and lemon peels. Just collect these leavings in a quart plastic bag in your fridge, and when you have a full bag, put them in a dark baking pan, fill with water to submerge, and leave in your cooker all day to simmer. Strain out the veggies and store the broth in your fridge or freezer.

**Beets** are versatile and nutritious. They can be blended into pestos and hummus, pureed in soup, and sliced or cubed for use in salads and bowls. They need to cook a long time (all day is ideal, but at least 4 hours), and it's easiest to cook them whole, with just the tops and tails trimmed off first. When a knife goes in easily, they're done. I've found it works pretty well to take a paper towel in my hand and use it to rub off the skin once the beet is cooked, and then I just compost the paper towel along with the skin. I like to cook up four beets at a time and have them on hand to slice into my lunch smoothie or onto a salad. They can also be peeled and sliced or diced before cooking to reduce the cooking time. Toss them with a little oil; no water required.

**Carrots** are another common root vegetable that's easy to cook to perfection with the sun. You can peel them or not, but if you're going to end up pureeing them in a hummus or a soup, cut them into short lengths or even dice them to speed up cooking. You can also cook them whole and serve them with a pat of butter or a splash of olive oil, some lemon juice, and some freshly chopped herbs. For this use, I like to leave them in the cooker all day so that they're really, really done.

**Celery root, parsnips, and rutabagas** are less commonly used root vegetables that are worth considering as fresh and nutrient-rich ingredients in pureed soups. They should be peeled and cut into chunks for most efficient cooking in the solar cooker.

**Onions and garlic** are also useful ingredients in pureed soups, peeled and cut into chunks before adding to the mix you're cooking. I like onions to be really well done when I use them in soups, so

# CUMIN-ROASTED CARROTS

**SERVES 4  |  COOK 4 to 5 hours**

*These work well as a side dish or added to bowls.*

4 large carrots, scrubbed and
    sliced on the diagonal into
    1/2-inch rounds
1 tablespoon olive oil
1 teaspoon maple syrup
1/2 teaspoon ground cumin
1/4 teaspoon salt

1.  Put the carrots, oil, maple syrup, cumin, and salt in a dark baking pan and mix well.
2.  Cover and bake in the solar cooker until tender when tested with a fork, 4 to 5 hours. To brown, uncover and allow to bake for another hour or so.

that means cooking them for at least 3 hours. For use in casseroles where varying ingredients need to bake in approximately the same time frame, I mince onions very fine to speed their cooking time. You can roast a whole head of garlic to use in hummus or infuse into oil. Cut off the top of the garlic head so the ends of the cloves are exposed. Put the head cut side up in a dark baking pan and cover. Bake in the solar cooker for 6 to 8 hours. Allow to cool and squeeze the cloves from the skins, starting from the root and working up.

**Potatoes**—red, yellow, Yukon Gold, russet—taste better and have a creamier texture when cooked with the sun than when cooked with any other method. They can be cooked whole in their skins in a dark baking pan—the more hours the better, but at least 4 hours—and peeled once they have cooled, or left unpeeled, for use in potato salads. For a faster turnaround (2 to 3 hours), you can peel and slice or cube the potatoes and toss with a little oil before cooking, since smaller pieces of food cook more quickly than larger pieces.

**Sweet potatoes** are among the all-stars of solar cuisine. I'm talking about the dark-skinned, orange-fleshed kind, sometimes sold in grocery stores labeled as yams or garnet yams. These sweet-tasting, good-for-you tubers can be used in spreads, soups, salads, bowls, casseroles, and desserts. For dishes that call for mashed sweet potato, you simply put one or two in a dark pan with skins on, cover, and cook for a few hours. When the flesh is soft, you scoop it out of the skin and use it in your recipe. For a full meal, cook up a batch of sweet potatoes this way to cut in half lengthwise and load up with black beans, grated cheese, sour cream, and sliced green onions and avocados.

For salads and bowls that require chunks of sweet potato, you want the flesh to hold its shape, so it's best to peel and

# MISO BUTTER POTATOES

**SERVES 4 | COOK 2 to 3 hours**

*This is an easy and tasty side dish to accompany fish and/or any kind of green salad.*

2 tablespoons butter
3 tablespoons mellow white miso
4 medium red potatoes,
    peeled, quartered, and sliced
    1/8-inch thick

1. Put the butter and miso in a dark baking pan, cover, and place in the solar cooker long enough to melt the butter.
2. Take the pan out of the cooker and stir the miso and butter together well. Add the potato slices and toss thoroughly to coat.
3. Cover and bake in the solar cooker until tender when tested with a fork, 2 to 3 hours.

cube the tuber before cooking and check it for doneness after 1 or 2 hours. If a dish calls for cooked sweet potato that's going to be pureed along with other cooked vegetables like onion, it's best to peel and chop the sweet potato first so it can be cooked right along with the other vegetable(s).

## SMOKY SWEET POTATOES

**SERVES 4  |  COOK 1 to 2 hours**

*These savory roasted sweet potatoes can be used to liven up bowls and salads. You can leave the skin on if you choose, but in that case scrub well before cubing.*

2 medium orange-fleshed sweet potatoes (also called yams), peeled and cut into 1/2-inch cubes
1 tablespoon olive oil
1 teaspoon smoked paprika
1/2 teaspoon salt

1.  Put the cubed sweet potatoes in a dark baking pan with the oil, paprika, and salt, and toss well.
2.  Cover and bake in the solar cooker until tender when tested with a fork, 1 to 2 hours.

## ABOVEGROUND VEGETABLES

Aboveground vegetables include the green leafies, the crucifers, and those vegetables that are actually fruits, defined botanically as growing from flowers and containing seeds (tomatoes, peppers, eggplant, squash, green beans). All of these take less time to cook with sunshine than root vegetables, but solar cooking does not preserve their bright colors or crispness. This doesn't matter if you blend these vegetables into soups, pestos, or spreads. Cooking aboveground vegetables with a little water in the roasting pan tends to mellow out the flavors, even though it's not strictly necessary.

**Asparagus** loses its bright green color but tastes fine when solar cooked until fork tender (1 to 2 hours).

**Bell peppers** can be cored, seeded, and cut up to cook with other veggies for pureed soups such as Chipotle Red Pepper Bisque. Their skin can be a little stringy if they aren't cooked long enough, 3 to 4 hours. They can also be stuffed with fillings containing bread crumbs, oatmeal, or cooked rice; chopped cooked meats and veggies; nuts and grated cheeses; chopped fresh herbs or sun-dried tomatoes; and fruits like apples, raisins, and apricots. You'll want to bake stuffed peppers for 4 to 5 hours or all day.

**Broccoli, cauliflower, and Brussels sprouts** can be baked with a little water in the bottom of the dark baking pan, but they need to cook for a very long time (4 to 5 hours) to become tender, and they lose their bright colors in the process. For this reason, you might want to solar cook them only when you plan to combine them in some other dish where color isn't so important, like Broccoli and Carrot Bisque.

**Corn** on the cob can be baked with or without the husk. The kernels may appear to shrink, but cooking with sunshine concentrates the sugars and makes for very sweet and juicy corn on the cob. If you husk the corn, put it in a dark baking pan and bake covered until the ears are steaming hot, 1 to 2 hours. Unhusked corn can be set on a dark baking sheet and covered with a dark cloth or barbecue mat and cooked for a similar amount of time.

**Eggplant**, peeled or unpeeled and cut into cubes, cooks in 2 to 3 hours and is delicious blended in Eggplant-Tahini Spread. Sliced eggplant can be used in solar-baked eggplant Parmesan but tastes better if it's started on the stove indoors, fried up in a little olive oil.

**Green beans** lose their bright green color when cooked with sunshine for long enough to get tender (2 to 3 hours), but this doesn't matter if you're going to blend them into Green Bean Pesto. Green beans cook and taste better when they're young and slender, but even older and tougher beans are good candidates for pesto. I once tried cooking frozen French green beans in a black roasting pan for an hour, and they came out perfectly, retaining their color even.

**Kale, chard, bok choy, and beet greens** can also be cooked with a little water in a dark baking pan for 2 to 3 hours and then dressed up with a little olive oil and some herbs to serve. They will lose their bright green color but retain their flavor.

**Rhubarb** is a green leafy vegetable used not for its leaves but for its reddish stems. Chop them into pieces and solar bake for about an hour to reach the point of tenderness, then blend with a sweetener and perhaps other fruit, as in Strawberry-Rhubarb Pudding and Rhubarb-Apple Topping Sauce.

**Spinach** is in a class by itself since it cooks so quickly. The recipe for Parmesan Spinach Polenta Bowl has you fold it in raw at the last minute, when the heat of the polenta is enough to wilt it sufficiently. You'll also find it used here in Spinach and Sun-Dried Tomato Frittata; Butternut Squash, Sun-Dried Tomato, and

Spinach Lasagna; and Zucchini, Carrot, and Spinach Lasagna. In those recipes it's a nice way to tuck in some greens that easily cook in the time the other ingredients need.

**Tomatoes** harvested from the garden or farmers market can be simmered all day in the solar cooker as a base for garden-fresh marinara. Tomatoes can also be simmered with other ingredients for use in pureed soups such as Shakshuka Tomato Soup or Tomato and Zucchini Bisque, or you can bake them.

**Winter squash** like butternut and acorn is easy to bake in a solar cooker. Just cut off the top, half lengthwise, and lay cut side down in a dark pan with a tight-fitting lid. You can scoop out the seeds after the flesh has cooked to softness, 1 to 2 hours. Or peel, cut lengthwise, seed, and slice thin to layer with other ingredients in a dish like Butternut Squash, Sun-Dried Tomato, and Spinach Lasagna.

**Zucchini squash** is so easily grown that I usually plant too much of it and at some point late in the summer find it piling up as I try to think of ways to eat it. Fortunately, it's so versatile it can be used in a variety of sun-baked dishes. It can be cut up and cooked with other veggies

for pureed soups like Zucchini and Carrot Soup, Tomato and Zucchini Bisque, or Zucchini and Fresh Basil Soup. It can be used sliced in Zucchini, Carrot, and Spinach Lasagna or grated in Carrot

## GARDEN-FRESH MARINARA

**MAKES 2 cups | COOK all day**

6 large or 9 medium tomatoes
1 medium onion, finely chopped
3 cloves garlic, minced
2 tablespoons olive oil
6-ounce can tomato paste
1 tablespoon finely chopped fresh oregano or 1 teaspoon dried oregano
1 tablespoon balsamic vinegar
1 teaspoon salt
1/4 teaspoon ground black pepper

1. Cut the tomatoes in half crosswise. Gently squeeze out the seeds and discard. (Don't worry if you don't get them all.) Dice the tomatoes and place them along with the onion, garlic, olive oil, tomato paste, oregano, balsamic vinegar, salt, and pepper in a dark baking pan.
2. Cover and cook all day in the solar cooker.

(or Zucchini) and Beet Brownies. It can also be cut lengthwise, seeded, and stuffed with fillings containing bread crumbs, oatmeal, or cooked rice; chopped cooked meats and veggies; nuts and grated cheeses; chopped fresh herbs or sun-dried tomatoes; and fruits like apples, raisins, and apricots. You'll want to bake stuffed zucchini for 2 to 3 hours.

## BAKED TOMATOES

**SERVES 4  |  COOK 1 to 2 hours**

4 medium tomatoes of any variety
1/4 cup cornmeal or almond meal
2 teaspoons olive oil
1/2 teaspoon seasoned salt
chopped fresh basil or chives

1. Cut the core out of each tomato and then slice off the top so you have a nice flat horizontal surface. Place cut side up in a dark baking pan.
2. In a small bowl, mix together the cornmeal or almond meal, olive oil, and salt. Top each tomato with 1/4 of the mixture and sprinkle with basil or chives.
3. Cover and bake in the solar cooker until soft, 1 to 2 hours.

## FRUIT

Fruit can be used in a variety of solar cooker recipes. Use **berries, peaches, plums, apricots, nectarines,** and/or **cherries** freshly harvested from the garden or farmers market in Summer Fruit Crumble or Summer Fruit Compote. **Pears** can be poached (Honey-Raspberry Poached Pears), and ripe mashed **bananas** can be incorporated into baked goods like Applesauce Oat Bread and Banana Peanut Butter Bars to add moisture and sweetness.

A bumper crop of **apples** can be used in many ways. You can core them, spoon in some granola, top with a pat of butter, and bake covered in a dark baking pan for 2 to 3 hours. Baked Apples with Cashew Cream is a fancier variation. Apples can be cooked with plums or rhubarb for Rhubarb-Apple Topping Sauce and Plum-Apple Topping Sauce. They can be cut up and cooked in Apple-Ginger Oat Pudding or made into applesauce, which in turn can serve as an ingredient in recipes like Applesauce Oat Bread and Lemon Shortcake Bars.

## WHOLE GRAINS

Solar cooking is a great method for preparing whole grains, which can be used in salads, bowls, and even desserts. It's a natural for grains like rice that don't like to be disturbed during cooking. Even grains that usually do need stirring, like polenta and oatmeal, can be cooked without stirring at the low temperatures generated in a solar cooker. The general rule of thumb here: use a little less water than on the stovetop and double the cooking time.

Grains should be cooked during the peak hours of sunlight, between 10 AM and 3 PM. Quinoa and buckwheat cook the fastest, brown rice the slowest. If you need to speed up cooking, boil the water first on the stovetop or in the solar cooker before adding to the grain. Be sure to check on grains, especially the quick-cooking ones, every 30 minutes or so to avoid overcooking.

**Rice** cooks in 2 to 4 hours, depending on the kind of rice. Use 1-3/4 cups broth or water to 1 cup of rice and cook covered. My favorite is brown jasmine rice because it comes out light and fluffy every time. Long-grain and basmati brown rice as well as black rice are also good bets. Short-grain brown rice is chewier, some might say gummier, so suit your own taste for such things. White rice cooks just fine, but brown rice is generally more nutritious.

Do be aware that research released by Consumer Reports in 2012 found measurable levels of arsenic in almost all of the rice varieties and products it tested, both organic and conventional. It found in follow-up studies that white basmati rice from California, India, and Pakistan,

## APPLESAUCE AS NATURE INTENDED

**MAKES 4 cups | COOK 3 to 4 hours or all day**

*Applesauce really needs no added sweetener. It's one of those dishes you can leave in the cooker all day long if need be. Try cooking it with 3 or 4 fresh sprigs of mint or rosemary, or add cinnamon to taste.*

6 Golden Delicious or Gala apples, peeled, quartered, cored, and coarsely chopped
1 lemon, cut in half

1. Place the apples in a dark baking pan and squeeze the lemon over them.
2. Cover and bake in the solar cooker until the apples are tender, 3 to 4 hours.
3. Mash the apples with a hand masher or fork. Leave them a little chunky if you prefer.

and sushi rice from the US on average has half of the arsenic of most other types of rice. Brown rice, because it retains its outer layers, contains more arsenic than white rice; brown basmati from California, India, and Pakistan has less arsenic than other brown rices. According to Consumer Reports, rinsing raw rice thoroughly before cooking and draining the excess water afterward can cut down on the arsenic content by about a third.

**Quinoa** cooks fast (an hour or less, 1-1/2 cups water to 1 cup quinoa) and can get a little scorched if left in the oven too long, so it needs careful tending. Also, it's recommended that you rinse and drain quinoa before cooking in order to lose the saponin coating that can taste bitter and also lead to leaky gut syndrome. I know it's a hassle finding a strainer with small enough mesh, but I was finally convinced to do it after learning of that health concern.

**Buckwheat** is another quick-cooking, high-protein, gluten-free grain; it gets mushy if cooked too long. Kasha is toasted buckwheat, which has a heartier flavor than the untoasted groats. I prefer the untoasted for Curried Buckwheat and Garbanzo Salad. Both cook in an hour or less; use 1-1/2 cups water to 1 cup buckwheat.

**Rolled oats** can be used in recipes like Applesauce Oat Bread, Black Bean Brownies, and Banana Peanut Butter Bars to impart a chewy texture and substitute for wheat flour. Quick oats are a little thinner than the standard variety; either variety can be used, as the oats have a

## CILANTRO-LIME RICE

SERVES 4  |  COOK 2 to 3 hours

1 cup brown jasmine or basmati rice, rinsed thoroughly
1-3/4 cups water or broth
1 tablespoon olive oil
1/2 teaspoon salt
1 lime, juice and zest
1/4 cup finely chopped fresh cilantro

1. Place the rice and water in a dark baking pan and stir well.
2. Cover and bake in the solar cooker until all the liquid has been absorbed, 2 to 3 hours. Remove from the cooker, fluff with a fork, and allow to cool.
3. Whisk together the oil, salt, lime juice, and lime zest, and pour over the rice. Add the cilantro and toss to mix well before serving.

chance to completely absorb the liquids in a recipe while the bread or brownies or bars are baking, 2 to 4 hours or more.

**Steel cut oats**, which have slightly more nutrients than other oat varieties, can be baked covered for 1 to 2 hours, with 2 cups liquid to 1 cup oats. They are featured here in Oat, Blueberry, and Cucumber Salad and in Apple-Ginger Oat Pudding.

**Polenta** and **grits** are both made of stone-ground dried corn kernels and are outstandingly easy to prepare in a solar cooker. They don't need stirring since they're cooking at such low temperatures, and they come out thick and creamy. They thicken more after cooking and can be served either before they set (Parmesan Spinach Polenta Bowl) or cut into squares after they set and topped with vegetables, marinara sauce, and/or meat. The basic recipe is 1 cup polenta or grits, 4 cups water, 2 tablespoons butter cut into little bits, and 1 teaspoon salt. Stir well, cover, and cook for 3 to 4 hours without disturbing.

**Bulgur wheat** should bake for at least an hour in the solar cooker, with 1-3/4 cups water to 1 cup bulgur. Bulgur contains gluten. If you avoid gluten, you can substitute quinoa for bulgur in tabouli; see the recipe for Quinoa Tabouli.

**Farro** (also called emmer) and **khorasan wheat** (sold as Kamut, ka-moot) are ancient grains that deliver more protein and fiber than either brown rice or whole-grain pasta. I also find them more flavorful than rice. Both contain gluten but less than modern wheat. Use 3 cups water to 1 cup pearled farro or Kamut; cover and bake for at least 2 hours and then drain.

**Barley** (which contains gluten) and **millet** (which does not) round out the whole grains that can be used in solar-cooked dishes. Use 2 cups water to 1 cup pearled barley; cover and bake for at least 2 hours. Use 1-3/4 cups water to 1 cup millet; cover and bake 1 to 2 hours.

**Whole-grain pasta** includes not only whole-wheat pasta these days but also pasta made from brown rice, barley, oats, and spelt (and then there are the bean-based pastas). You can bake any kind of pasta with other ingredients in a solar cooker without boiling the pasta first. It goes in raw and soaks up liquid from the other ingredients as the dish cooks slowly and gently. For mac and cheese, the key is to cut the sauce with water, which the uncooked macaroni will sop up as it cooks. You can also use this method to cook tortellini, substituting a sauce and toppings of your choice. For some other ideas using pasta, try Butternut Squash, Sun-Dried Tomato, and Spinach Lasagna; Zucchini, Carrot, and Spinach Lasagna; and Ziti Baked with Three Cheeses and Fresh Herbs.

# EASY MAC AND CHEESE

**SERVES 4 | COOK 3 to 4 hours**

1-1/4 cups prepared Alfredo sauce
1-1/4 cups water
2 cups uncooked whole-grain
   elbow macaroni
1 tablespoon olive oil
1 cup grated cheddar cheese
1/4 cup seasoned bread crumbs

1. In a large bowl, whisk the Alfredo sauce and the water until smooth. Pour the macaroni into the bottom of a dark baking pan and toss well with the oil. Pour the watered-down Alfredo sauce over it and stir to mix.
2. Cover and bake in the solar cooker until the macaroni is as tender as you'd like and the sauce is bubbly, at least 3 hours.
3. Half an hour before serving, sprinkle the cheese and bread crumbs evenly over the top. Put back in the cooker uncovered until the cheese melts.

## LEGUMES

**Lentils** are solar cooking all-stars. Dried lentils don't need to be soaked before cooking, and they take half as long as dried beans to cook, 2 or 3 hours usually. They're full of protein (18 grams per cooked cup, compared to 14.5 grams per cup of cooked beans and 9 grams per cup of cooked quinoa) and fiber. They're versatile enough to be used in all sorts of dishes, including spreads, salads, and bowls.

Different types of lentils have different qualities, but the proportions for cooking are always the same: 1 cup of lentils to 2 cups of water. The small black lentils known as belugas hold their shape best and are used in Black Lentil Salad with Smoked Trout and Red Peppers. Brown or green lentils hold their shape next best and are used in Green Lentil Salad with Edamame, Grapes, and Feta; Sesame-Ginger Lentil and Quinoa Salad; and Greek Lentil Bowl. Red lentils get mushy, which makes them perfect for dips and spreads like Chipotle Lentil Hummus.

**Beans** like adzuki beans, great northerns, black beans, and garbanzos are great to have on hand for use in salads, casseroles, bowls, and even desserts (like Black Bean Brownies). I usually prefer the convenience of using canned beans and have indicated their use in recipes in this book, but you can certainly use dried beans cooked in the solar cooker instead. It just adds an extra day of prep time for some meals. A 15-ounce can of beans contains 1-1/2 cups, which is the yield if you cook 4 ounces (about 1/2 cup) of most types of dried beans.

Note that beans contain lectins, proteins that bind to carbohydrates, which can cause stomach upset and digestive issues if the beans aren't thoroughly cooked. Lectins are deactivated by boiling, a process that canned beans go through. Solar-cooked beans do reach and exceed the boiling point—212 degrees F. Dried beans cook at different rates depending on how old they are. Garbanzos need to cook longer than other beans to become tender and are sturdier in general.

Soaking dried beans in water before cooking them shortens the cooking time and prevents the skins from bursting before the beans are tender. Pick through dried beans for stones and debris, rinse them in a colander, then place them in a dark pan or pot. Cover them with water and let them sit overnight or for at least 6 hours. Drain off the soaking water and cover the beans with fresh water to 2 inches above their surface. Cover the pan or pot and bake in the solar cooker for 6

to 8 hours until soft. Drain and use or refrigerate.

## POULTRY AND MEAT

**Chicken** is among the easier foods to cook with sunshine and comes out moist, tender, and flavorful. Cook it ahead to have on hand for salads, bowls, and casseroles. It's super simple: open a package of chicken breasts or thighs, pop them right into a dark baking pan, cover, and cook for 1 to 2 hours. The meat is easy to separate from fat and connective tissue once it's been baked.

If you're going to shred or cube the chicken for use in another dish, you can use skin-on, bone-in breasts, thighs, or drumsticks. Leaving the skin on will keep the meat moister as it bakes, and it's easy enough to pull off the skin while you're taking the meat from the bones.

For recipes that call for chicken to bake in some kind of sauce, use skinless and boneless breasts or thighs. Solar baking chicken releases a lot of juices, so cut back on the liquid to allow for that. Alternatively, you can bake the chicken for an hour and then drain off the juices (saving to use in recipes that call for chicken broth) before adding the sauce.

**Beef**, **pork**, and **lamb** benefit from slow cooking and can be left in the cooker

# BARBACOA BEEF

**SERVES 4 to 6  |  COOK 6 to 8 hours**

*This flavorful pulled chuck meat can be used in tacos, burritos, tostadas, and salads. See the recipe for Barbacoa Burrito Bowl.*

**Into the cooker:**
1-1/2 pounds chuck roast that's been trimmed of fat and cut into 2-inch chunks
1 small red onion, minced
2 cloves garlic, minced
1 chipotle from a can of chipotle peppers in adobo sauce, chopped, or 1/2 teaspoon chipotle chili powder
2 tablespoons fresh lime juice
1 tablespoon apple cider vinegar
1 tablespoon chopped fresh oregano or 1 teaspoon dried oregano
1/2 teaspoon salt
1/4 teaspoon ground black pepper

1. Place the meat, onion, garlic, chipotle pepper or powder, lime juice, vinegar, oregano, salt, and pepper in a dark baking pan and stir well.
2. Cover and bake in the solar cooker until the beef is tender, 6 hours or longer.
3. Shred with two forks and mix well with the juices in the pan.

all day, only becoming more tender. The best cuts of meat to use are chuck roast, beef brisket, and short ribs; pork shoulder or butt; and lamb shanks. Brush the meat with a little oil to seal in the juices and bake in a dark roasting pan with a lid, allowing at least an hour of cooking time per pound. Beef or pork can be shredded—or "pulled"—after cooking all day in the solar cooker.

## SEAFOOD

**Fish** (salmon, sole, tilapia, halibut, and trout are good candidates) and **shellfish** (such as shrimp and scallops, my top two shellfish picks for health and flavor) are at their best cooked slowly and gently to retain moisture, so solar cooking is the ideal method to prepare them. They cook quickly, 1 to 2 hours or less in full sun, and you don't want to overcook them, so plan to keep an eye on them. Cook covered and check every 30 minutes. Fish flakes easily with a fork when it's done; scallops turn milky white or opaque and firm; shrimp turns opaque pink and firm, and is overcooked when it curls up into an O.

Fresh seafood is best, if you're lucky enough to live near a seacoast, but frozen also works. Frozen shell-on shrimp that's been deveined is the ideal kind for solar cooking. Shrimp shells should be left on for cooking, as they contribute to the flavor that develops and give the shrimp a plumper texture. They also keep the shrimp from immediately going from perfectly cooked to overcooked. Remove frozen fish or shellfish from packaging and thaw in the refrigerator overnight before cooking.

## MISO BAKED SALMON

**SERVES 4 | COOK 1 to 2 hours**

*Use this baked salmon in salads, bowls, or tacos, or eat as is, accompanied by Corn and Blueberry Salad and/or Sour Cream Dill Potato Salad.*

1 pound salmon fillets, rinsed and
    patted dry
2 tablespoons white miso
2 tablespoons water
1 teaspoon toasted sesame oil
1–2 cloves garlic, minced
1 teaspoon minced fresh ginger

1. Oil a dark baking pan and place the salmon in it skin-side down.
2. Whisk together the miso, water, sesame oil, garlic, and ginger into a smooth paste, then spoon and spread over the salmon.
3. Cover and bake in the solar cooker until the fish flakes easily with a fork, 1 to 2 hours.

Rinse fish and shellfish and pat dry before placing in a dark baking pan that you've oiled or melted butter in (maybe mixed with oil). Turn the fish or shellfish over in the oil or butter and flavor with seasoning rubs and toppings. Fresh herbs such as basil, thyme, rosemary, tarragon, dill, or mint can be chopped and sprinkled over. Or try topping fish with a mixture of sun-dried tomatoes, kalamata olives, capers, and artichoke hearts. Alternatively, you can marinate fish or shellfish in teriyaki sauce overnight, or prepare a melted butter, lemon juice, and parsley sauce to go on top once the fish or shellfish has been taken out of the cooker.

## EGGS AND CHEESE

Quiches and frittatas are easy to put together and love being baked gently with sunshine. Standard flour crusts tend to get soggy, so you need to be a little creative. Either go crustless or try something like the crust made of tortillas for Green Chili Quiche or walnut pieces for Pear and Gorgonzola Quiche. A basic quiche recipe for four to six people uses 6 eggs to 1 cup of plain unsweetened nondairy milk, half and half, cream, sour cream, buttermilk, or plain Greek yogurt. Sprinkle some cooked vegetables or uncooked spinach in a dark 9-3/4-inch-round roaster, crumble or shred 2 cups (8 ounces) of cheese over all, and pour the egg mixture in. Cook 1 to 2 hours; be careful not to overcook.

Any dish that requires you to melt cheese can be prepared in a solar cooker. Open-faced toasted cheese sandwiches or mini pizzas on English muffins are just two of many possible ideas. Allow 1/2 hour at the peak of sunshine for cheese topping to melt.

You can also hard boil eggs in a solar cooker. To see if eggs are hard cooked, twirl them on a hard surface like your kitchen counter. If they spin fast, they're cooked. Until you get a feeling for how long eggs take to hard boil in your circumstances, it's best to err on the side of leaving them in too long. Place raw eggs in a dark pan and cover with water. Cover the pan and bake for about 4 hours during the hours of peak sun (10 AM to 3 PM). Remove and immerse in cold water before peeling.

## NUTS AND SEEDS

Nuts and seeds make great snacks and garnishes, and it's easy to bake nut and seed mixes in the solar cooker. Bake them uncovered in a dark sheet pan if you're using a Haines panel cooker, where the flexible plastic insulating shell stands off the pan so air can circulate and steam can escape, or a box cooker with the lid propped open slightly to allow the steam to escape. If using an oven bag in a panel cooker, you can turn a black 9-by-13-inch roasting pan upside down over the sheet pan to hold the heat in and prevent the oven bag from collapsing on the food. See the recipe for Spicy Chocolate Nuts, and also try this one.

## SPICED SEEDS

**MAKES 2 cups | COOK 2 to 3 hours**

*I like throwing these into salads or sprinkling on cold soups. A handful also makes a good midafternoon snack.*

1 cup raw sunflower seeds
1 cup raw pumpkin seeds
1 tablespoon olive oil
1–1/2 tablespoons honey
1/2 teaspoon salt
1/8 teaspoon cayenne pepper
1 teaspoon ground cumin
1/2 teaspoon cinnamon

1. In a large bowl, mix all the ingredients with your hands until the seeds are evenly coated.
2. Oil a dark baking sheet with a slight rim and spread the mixture evenly on it. Bake uncovered in the solar cooker until the seeds are dry, 2 to 3 hours.
3. Allow to cool before storing in a glass container at room temperature.

## BAKING BREAD

You can bake just about any kind of bread in the solar cooker—quick breads, yeast breads, fruit breads, biscuits, muffins, scones—as long as you bake on a clear day during the hours of peak sun (10 AM to 3 PM). Dark loaf pans are best at converting light into heat, but you can use a clear glass loaf pan placed on a dark surface and covered with a dark pan or grill mat. Cooking time depends on the color of the dough (darker cooks faster), the size of the loaf pan, the number of loaves you're baking, and the number of times you refocus the cooker. Generally, breads bake in 2 to 4 hours.

Bread bakes more quickly if it's covered because steam from uncovered bread will fog up your box cooker window or oven bag and cut down on the sun's rays reaching the bread. You can also bake the bread uncovered and prop the lid or oven bag open slightly to allow the steam to escape. This isn't a problem with the Haines panel cooker, as the flexible plastic insulating shell stands well off the food. If you're using a panel cooker with an oven bag, try laying a grill mat over the loaf pan to hold in the heat and prevent the oven bag from collapsing on the food.

If you find that the top of the bread gets done before the rest of it, try lining the bottom of your loaf pan with waxed paper and turning the loaf out after a couple of hours. Then place it back in the pan upside down and continue baking to dry out the bottom. ☀

*Relax, dinner's in the solar cooker.*

# Resources

## WEBSITES

The Solar Cookers International (SCI) Solar Cooking Wiki (solarcooking.org or solarcooking.fandom.com) is the most comprehensive and up-to-date online source of solar cooker information, plans, and links to models for sale.

SCI has developed a scientific procedure to measure the performance of various solar cooker models. View results of its performance evaluation process (PEP) at solarcookers.org/work/research/results.

The Solar Cooker at CantinaWest site created by Nathan Parry (solarcooker-at-cantinawest.com) also offers a wealth of information about solar cooking, although it is no longer maintained.

Additional information about solar cookers and solar cooking can be found on the websites of various inventors and producers of solar cookers. These include the following:

- oursuncooks.com (Sharon Clausson, the Copenhagen solar cooker)

- hainessolarcookers.com (Roger Haines, the Haines 2.0 solar cooker)
- solcook.com (Jim La Joie, the All Season Solar Cooker)
- she-inc.org (Solar Household Energy, the HotPot solar cooker)
- sunoven.com (Sun Ovens International, the All American Sun Oven)
- sunbdcorp.com (Sun BD Corporation, the SunFocus Solar Electric Oven)
- sunok.eu (SunOK, the Suntaste solar cooker)

YouTube has numerous helpful videos about solar cooking. Just search on the term "solar cooking."

## BOOKS AND BOOKLETS

Anderson, Lorraine, and Rick Palkovic. *Cooking with Sunshine*. Cambridge, MA: Da Capo Press, 2006. Although some sections are dated, this comprehensive guide to solar cuisine describes the history of solar cooking and how to build panel and box cookers, and includes 150 easy recipes.

Fodor, Eben. *The Solar Food Dryer*. Gabriola Island, BC: New Society Publishers, 2005. This is a good primer on harvesting the sun's energy for drying (or cooking) food, with sun path charts and other useful solar data.

Hawken, Paul, ed. *Drawdown: The Most Comprehensive Plan Ever Proposed to Reverse Global Warming*. New York: Penguin Books, 2017. This well-researched compendium presents the hundred most substantive solutions to reverse global warming, all solutions that are already being implemented and can easily be scaled up. The solution ranked #4 is a plant-rich diet, and the solution ranked #21 is clean cookstoves. "Solar cookers are an exceedingly clean option."

Pollan, Michael. *Cooked: A History of Transformation*. New York: Penguin, 2013. Pollan argues that reclaiming cooking as an act of enjoyment and self-reliance may be the single most important step anyone can take to help make the American food system healthier and more sustainable.

Robbins, Ocean. *31-Day Food Revolution: Heal Your Body, Feel Great, and Transform Your World*. New York: Grand Central Publishing, 2019. Ocean and his dad, John Robbins, run the Food Revolution Network, foodrevolution.org, which is "committed to healthy, ethical, and sustainable food for all." Check out the blog for ongoing information supporting healthy people and a healthy planet.

*Solar Cookers: How to Make, Use, and Enjoy*, 10th ed. (58 pages, 2004) from Solar Cookers International can be downloaded free from solarcooking.org/plans/plans.pdf. It shows how to make panel and box cookers and also gives recipes, tips, and a brief history of solar cooking.

Tickell, Josh. *Kiss the Ground: How the Food You Eat Can Reverse Climate Change, Heal Your Body, and Ultimately Save Our World*. New York: Simon and Schuster, 2017. Documentary filmmaker Tickell explores how regenerative agriculture can turn around our cascading environmental crises—and how our food choices can support this process.

Ulivieri, Nicola. *Solar Cookers: Cooking with the Sun, History, Theory, Construction, Recipes*. Self-published, 2019. If you want to know more about the history and theory of solar cooking, this book by an Italian engineer will satisfy your curiosity.

## ORGANIZATIONS

Solar Cookers International (solarcookers. org) has since 1987 been spreading the gospel of solar cooking in developing nations. By promoting solar cooking among vulnerable populations worldwide, it aims to improve human health, economic well-being, the lives of women, and the environment.

Solar Household Energy (she-inc. org), founded in 1998, works with nongovernmental organizations and entrepreneurs to leverage the power of solar cooking to improve social, economic and environmental conditions in sun-rich areas around the world.

Slow Food (slowfood.com) is a global grassroots organization founded in 1989 to prevent the disappearance of local food cultures and traditions, counteract the rise of fast life, and combat people's dwindling interest in the food they eat, where it comes from, and how our food choices affect the world around us. The Slow Food Climate Pledge acknowledges that one of the main causes of climate change is the industrial model of food production and consumption. ☀

# Many Thanks

To compile this book, I took existing recipes and tinkered with them until they were simple to prepare, tasted good to me, and worked in the solar cooker. I got many of my recipe ideas by roaming around online and in cookbooks, so I want to thank all of those foodie bloggers and writers who put together new food ideas and tastes. I'm very grateful to Philip Lew for taste testing the recipes, editorial review, and for patiently photographing plates before sitting down to eat. I'm also grateful to the solar cooker inventors who gifted me with their cookers for testing—Roger Haines, Sharon Clausson, and Jim La Joie. I thank Jamie Knapp, Beeara Edmonds, Megan Anderson, Robyn Boyd, and Pauline Presson for testing recipes. Thanks to my writing pals Carla Wise and Carol Savonen for offering feedback and encouragement. Special thanks to Ash Good for making the book beautiful and gently keeping me on a timeline. Most of all, I give thanks for our sun, the ultimate power source from which all blessings flow. ☀

# Recipe Index

# Index

# C

# About the Author

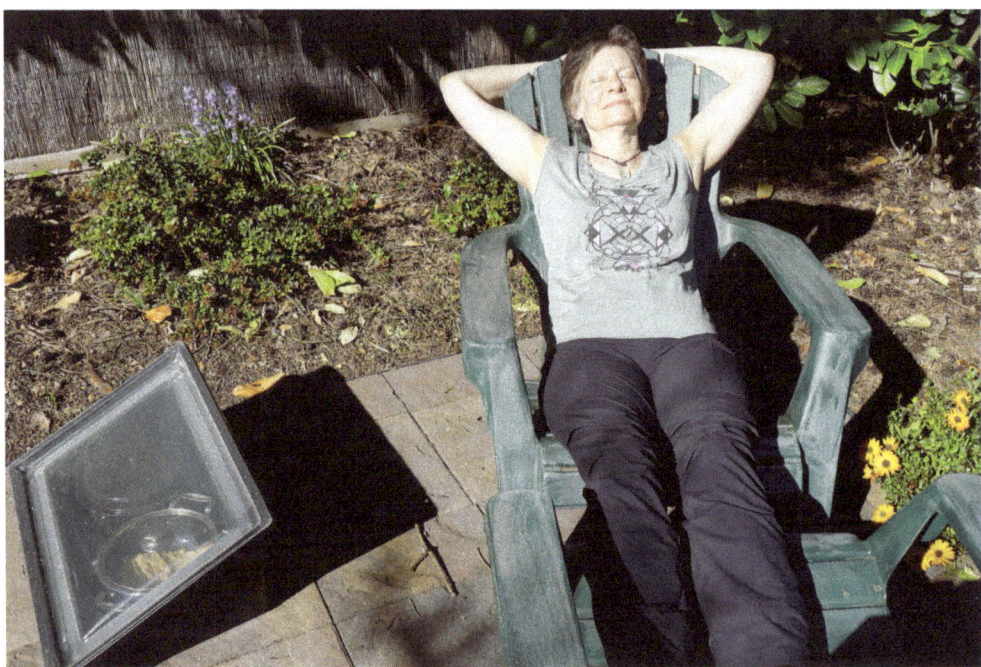

**LORRAINE ANDERSON** stumbled across the magic of solar cooking at the California State Fair in 1991 and has never looked back. All the summertime meals at the home she shares with photographer Philip M. Lew are prepared in a solar cooker. She coauthored *Cooking with Sunshine* (with Rick Palkovic) and has edited dozens of books encouraging Earth consciousness, including her own compilations *Sisters of the Earth* and *Earth & Eros*.

www.ingramcontent.com/pod-product-compliance
Lightning Source LLC
Chambersburg PA
CBHW041140120626
46547CB00020B/3054